COLLEGE STUD

D0792857

101 Ways to Score Higher on Your SAT Reasoning Exam

By Rebekah Sack

College Study Hacks: 101 Ways to Score Higher on Your SAT Reasoning Exam

Copyright © 2017 Atlantic Publishing Group, Inc.
1405 SW 6th Avenue • Ocala, Florida 34471 • Phone 800-814-1132 • Fax 352-622-1875
Website: www.atlantic-pub.com • Email: sales@atlantic-pub.com
SAN Number: 268-1250

Library of Congress Cataloging-in-Publication Data

Names: Sack, Rebekah, 1994- author.
Title: College study hacks : 101 ways to score higher on your SAT reasoning
  exam / by Rebekah Sack.
Description: Ocala, Florida : Atlantic Publishing Group, Inc., [2017] |
  Includes bibliographical references and index.
Identifiers: LCCN 2017009994 (print) | LCCN 2017016424 (ebook) | ISBN
  9781620230787 (ebook) | ISBN 9781620230626 (pbk) | ISBN 9781620232439 (library binding)
Subjects: LCSH: SAT (Educational test)--Study guides. | Reasoning--Ability
  testing.
Classification: LCC LB2353.57 (ebook) | LCC LB2353.57 .S1955 2017 (print) |
  DDC 378.1/662--dc23
LC record available at https://lccn.loc.gov/2017009994

Printed in the United States

PROJECT MANAGER AND EDITOR: Rebekah Sack • rsack@atlantic-pub.com
INTERIOR LAYOUT: Antoinette D'Amore • addesign@videotron.ca

Printed on Recycled Paper

Reduce. Reuse.
RECYCLE.

A decade ago, Atlantic Publishing signed the Green Press Initiative. These guidelines promote environmentally friendly practices, such as using recycled stock and vegetable-based inks, avoiding waste, choosing energy-efficient resources, and promoting a no-pulping policy. We now use 100-percent recycled stock on all our books. The results: in one year, switching to post-consumer recycled stock saved 24 mature trees, 5,000 gallons of water, the equivalent of the total energy used for one home in a year, and the equivalent of the greenhouse gases from one car driven for a year.

Over the years, we have adopted a number of dogs from rescues and shelters. First there was Bear and after he passed, Ginger and Scout. Now, we have Kira, another rescue. They have brought immense joy and love not just into our lives, but into the lives of all who met them.

We want you to know a portion of the profits of this book will be donated in Bear, Ginger and Scout's memory to local animal shelters, parks, conservation organizations, and other individuals and nonprofit organizations in need of assistance.

– Douglas & Sherri Brown,
President & Vice-President of Atlantic Publishing

Table of Contents

Chapter 3
Preparation 101: The Countdown to the Test 47

Chapter 4
SAT Prep: Plan Your Attack 57

Chapter 5
Develop Your Strategies 69

Chapter 6
Math Strategies: Winning the Numbers Game

Chapter 7
Writing Strategies: Crafting the Winning Essay

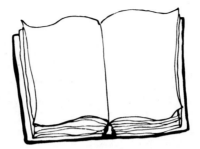

Introduction

There are a lot of serious things that people argue about in the world — politics, religion, mint chocolate chip or cookies and cream — and test-taking is no exception. People argue that tests are useless because students forget everything they learned as soon as the test is over. Others wonder how you can measure a person's intelligence without them. Still others question whether test results have anything to do with intelligence at all.

Well, the argument definitely isn't over, but at least for now, the world we live in still relies pretty heavily on test results. The majority of colleges recommend submitting an SAT score with your application, and many even deem it a mandatory requirement. The SAT is pretty much the standard (along with the ACT) as far as college admissions are concerned.

Many colleges rely on that number to determine your potential success. The test covers the three subjects that are thought of as the most crucial for college success: reading, writing, and math. If you're already a pro at test taking and you can read, write, and calculate your way to the top, then high-fives to you. But, if the thought of taking a test makes you want to ninja mode right out of the classroom and the letters x and y make you queasy, this book is going to be your new long lost love. Or best friend. Or just a good study resource.

You may be wondering how it's possible to fill up an entire book on the SAT, but get ready. You are about to be 101 steps closer to your highest score ever! But, before we get started, let's meet our SAT experts that will be featured throughout the book with tips and tricks to make your life *so* much easier.

Guest Features

Alexandra McIlvaine
Director of Education, Educational Services

I first took the SAT when I was a sophomore in high school in 2000, then again in 2001 after receiving tutoring with Educational Services (ES). After graduating from college with my Bachelors in Education, I started teaching at Educational Services in the spring of 2008 while I obtained my Masters in Education. What began as part-time work evolved into my full-time career, and I have been teaching the SAT and a plethora of other standardized tests ever since. As it is customary for Educational Services instructors to take the SAT in the test center with our students, I have taken the SAT countless times over the years in the original 1600 format, the 2400 format and the new 1600 format to better understand any subtle changes made to the content of the test material, and to be able to relate well to our students.

Clark Steen
Tutor, Power Forward Tutoring

I have been teaching SATs since 1999, first with Princeton Review, and then as the owner of Power Forward Tutoring from 2001 to the present. I teach and take tests for a living. I have taken the SAT, ACT, SAT Subject Tests for Math, Literature, both World and American History, The DAT, LSAT, MCAT, GRE, and GMAT. I always score within the top 1-2 percent.

Tom Rose
CEO, Testive

I've been teaching the SAT heavily since 2011. That's the year I graduated MIT and founded Testive. Testive was built using technology that I developed while at MIT to speed up the learning process. An independent MIT study found that using our approach, students improved their scores 100 points in seven days. (This was on the old 2400-point scale. This is the equivalent of 66 points in seven days in the new 1600-point scale.)

I have personally taken the official SAT in 2000 and 2014. I've also taken a zillion unofficial practice tests every year for the last five years.

Alexis Browsh
Teacher and Private Tutor, Ready Tutors

Alexis Browsh is a history teacher and the owner and lead tutor at Ready Tutors, a Philadelphia-area tutoring service that employs certified, experienced tutors for in-home support and test prep across all subject areas. In addition to coaching students preparing for a variety of standardized tests, Browsh proctors exams, provides testing accommodations, and counsels college-bound students in the application and essay-writing process.

CHAPTER 1

Test Basics: Know the Enemy

I f the SAT makes you want to puke everywhere, you're probably being a little dramatic. But seriously, the SAT can be really daunting. A lot of people get caught up on the idea that this one number is the only gateway to their goals, and if that number isn't right on target, well...the dream is dead.

It's true that your performance on the SAT Reasoning Test is a key factor in admissions and scholarship decisions at most colleges and universities. It's no secret that this test is important. However, you don't want to go totally nuts while you're preparing for it.

This book is going to teach you two things: you're going to learn how to improve your score with some awesome strategies, and you're going to learn how to stay calm and collected.

The SAT is pretty brutal. It demands incredible stamina, knowledge, and determination. I mean, four hours of extreme concentration is … well, it's brutal! The first thing you need to do in order to arm yourself for this test is to know what to expect. And that means not asking your mom and dad.

1 Meet the New SAT

In most things, listening to the wisdom of your parents might get you somewhere. When it comes to the SAT, though, asking for advice from someone who took the test even a few years ago is useless. The test is constantly changing, and March of 2016 marked a complete overhaul to the beast.

Back in the day, the test had just one math section and one "verbal" section with vocabulary and reading-comprehension questions. Then, the test evolved to include a third section: writing. The new test dropped most of the vocabulary parts, such as analogies, and it focused more on grammar. It added an essay. Simultaneously, it had more sections and was longer. Then, the SAT was again completely redone, and it became one of the longest tests many students would ever take.

Guest Feature: Clark Steen

The new SAT was formed out of panic. As of 2012, the ACT has more test takers than the SAT. Few colleges were taking the SAT, and entire systems — such as those in Texas and California — were threatening to stop accepting the SAT, and other schools simply went test-optional. SAT fired its president and hired the former president of ACT to redesign the new SAT in a bid to remain relevant. Over a three-year span, the new SAT was made into a five-section test, including the optional essay, and most of the material is exactly the same as that on the ACT, unsurprisingly.

One of the most important things to know about the new 2016 SAT is that it is long — nearly four hours. Here's a quick peek at what it looks like:

Test time	3 hours + a 50-minute optional essay
Structure	3 tests + an optional essay
Number of questions	154
Time per question	1 minute, 10 seconds
Score range	Composite 400-1600

It's also important to know how much time you'll be spending with each category:

- Reading: 65 minutes
- Writing and Language: 35 minutes
- Math: 80 minutes

Knowing what to expect is half the battle. At least now you have a little bit of ammunition.

2 Know What's at Stake

The SAT is the country's largest college entrance exam, although another test, the ACT, tends to be prominent in much of the Midwest. You can see the difference between the two tests here: **https://collegereadiness. collegeboard.org/sat/inside-the-test/compare-new-sat-act.**

For decades, the SAT has helped colleges and universities sort out applicants and decide who to accept from the flood of applying students. For most of that time, it was called the Scholastic Aptitude Test. That is because what it measures(or what it's supposed to measure) is how successful you are likely to be in college, or your "aptitude" for success. Although the test still measures this, the College Board pulled the reference to "aptitude" from the SAT name — a move that critics of the test saw as an admission that it does not measure what it is supposed to measure. Since 1993, the letters "SAT" have stood for nothing, much like Kentucky Fried Chicken changed their name to KFC to distance themselves from the word "fried."

Critics argue that the SAT is not really that useful in predicting college success. They say it does not measure many skills that are important, such as persistence, the ability to work well in a group, or even knowledge of specific academic concepts. In an ideal world, universities could interview each student — in addition to considering grades, recommendations, and test scores — before deciding which applicants would fit in best at their institutions. But with so many students trying to get in, it's just not practical. This limitation explains why the SAT first became widely used during the 1950s, when the GI Bill allowed thousands of former World War II soldiers to go to college for free, flooding universities with applications. With applicants from all over the country, it was hard to tell whether an "A" meant the same thing everywhere. The SAT gave schools a quick, standardized way to compare students, and it still does.

What does all this mean for you? First of all, it should help you understand the role of the test in the admissions process. The SAT is crucially important, as it's often your first impression. However, if you're not so great at taking tests — and most people know pretty well by high school whether they are — you also want to make the most of the other tools admissions offices use:

- Keep your grades up
- Take part in extracurricular activities
- Take on leadership roles
- Consider taking the ACT
- Write a stellar entrance essay
- Do volunteer work

Also keep in mind that smaller colleges and universities have a smaller pool of applicants and can spend more time evaluating each application, so they may put less weight on the SAT.

Getting a good score on the SAT is important for obvious reasons, but know what's at stake here. Yes, the SAT is a very important tool in college admissions. Yes, it may affect whether you get into a particular college or university. But it does not determine how "smart" you are, whether you will be successful later in life, or even how well you will do in college. So do your best, but do not let the results — good or bad — change how you think of yourself or your abilities.

3   Know the 2016 SAT

As you already know, the SAT is constantly changing. Your teachers can tell you what the SAT was like when they took it, but odds are, their advice is going to be outdated.

There are three main sections:

- Reading Test
- Writing and Language Test
- Math Test

There is also an optional essay component, which some colleges require — it's a safe bet to go ahead and take the essay portion so that you can be fully armed when applying to your ideal schools (in case they require it).

Now that you know the basic layout of the test, here is what's different about it as of 2016.

Context

The College Board realizes that you aren't going to know every single word you've written down on a flashcard. The new SAT focuses more on words in context so that you can determine what a word means more easily and practically. Many of the new questions will ask you to determine a word's meaning based on context clues.

Evidence

Every section of the exam has a greater focus on evidence-based observations. You will be asked to look at charts, graphics, and chunks of text. Then, you will be expected to choose the best answer based on the evidence you could find in those bits.

The SAT Essay is the same way — after reading a passage, you'll be asked to figure out how the writer built his or her argument in order to persuade you. What evidence did they use? Many of the SAT scorers will be looking for clear, well-thought out evidence.

Analyzing

Similar to evidence, the SAT Essay will ask you to do a lot of analyzing. The College Board is trying to help you learn how to be a better reader, so they ask you to analyze bits of writing. You'll be looking for things like evidence, reasoning, and stylistic and persuasive elements.

Math

The Math Test covers three main sections:

1. Problem Solving and Data Analysis
2. Heart of Algebra
3. Passport to Advanced Math

Problem Solving and Data Analysis includes the following elements:

- Ratios
- Percentages
- Proportional reasoning to solve problems in science, social science, and career contexts

The Heart of Algebra focuses on:

- Linear equations and systems
- Abstraction

The Passport to Advanced Math covers:

- Complex equations
- The manipulation that complex equations require

The math section will also cover other math topics, such as geometry and trigonometry, all in the hopes that the test will mirror skills that are relevant in many careers today.

Guest Feature: Clark Steen

The first section is Reading, which no longer has the sentence completions portion. The SAT announced that they would be vastly decreasing the amount of vocabulary on the test, but they simply placed the vocabulary liberally throughout the Reading passages. The answer choices are still tricky.

The second section is Grammar, which is very similar to that of the ACT, and has switched over to Turabian (Chicago Manual of Style) rather than MLA. In addition, the SAT wanted an element similar to that found in the Science section of the ACT, so they added charts, graphs, and tables to the Reading and Grammar sections, which seems incongruous.

The third section is Math without calculator, and the fourth is Math with calculator. We have found that a calculator is crucial on section three and mostly unnecessary on the fourth. The SAT got rid of virtually nothing, keeping the Student Produced Responses, which are the questions that do not have answer choices — the ones that students seem to universally loathe.

However, the SAT did reduce to four answer choices on the entire test (the ACT still has five in the Math section), as well as getting rid of the one-quarter point guessing penalty.

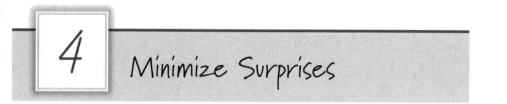

4 Minimize Surprises

You shouldn't be surprised when you open the test booklet. Back in tip No. 1, we took a look at how the overall test was structured. It's 154 questions, and the thing is three hours long. Take a look at this chart to see how those three hours are broken up among the test components.

The Post-March-2016 SAT		
Component	**Time Allotted (in minutes)**	**# of Questions/ Tasks**
Reading	65	52
Writing and Language	35	44
Essay (optional)	50	1
Math	80	58
Total	180 (230 with essay)	154 (155 with essay)

Take a look at this chart and really come to terms with how the test is going to be divided. We will get into more specific details later on, but having a clear idea of what to expect in terms of format is a good starting place.

5 Start Studying

Along the way, you might run into someone who says, "You can't study for the SAT. Don't waste your time."

Back away slowly.

It's true that the SAT is not *designed* to be a test you study for. It is designed to be much like an IQ test so that no amount of studying should change your score. But decades of test-score analysis have shown that students who study do better. Research also shows that for every hour you study, you can expect to gain an average of about 3 test points[1]. It is recommended that you take an initial practice test to see where you stand, and then figure out how much catching up you need to do. Khan Academy, partner of The College Board, offers official, full-length SAT practice exams here: **www.khanacademy.org/sat**.

A lot of the studying you will be doing is learning what will be on the SAT and figuring out which skills you need to perfect. Even the ones who never study for anything and always get a perfect score — don't look at me — will benefit from reviewing material before test day.

---

1 Lindsay, 2015.

Guest Feature: Alexandra McIlvaine

The most important piece of advice I remember receiving was "practice makes perfect." As cliché as it sounds, I took the advice to heart; I was able to raise my score over 300 points (on the 1600 scale) when I took the time to review each of my errors with my instructor at Educational Services.

CHAPTER 2

Your Score: Understanding the Numbers

The SAT has a lot of important qualities, but if we're being honest, most of us will admit that one part matters above all others: the score. Yes, well-meaning friends and family will tell you that you should "just do your best," and they're right. But keep in mind that the only reason you're taking this test is to have a brag-worthy score that will impress potential colleges. It's a good idea to know what kind of number the colleges and universities you hope to attend will be looking for.

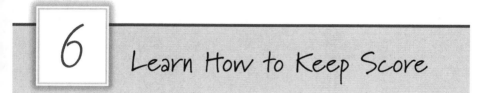

6 Learn How to Keep Score

We already know why we need to do our best on the SAT and how colleges will use our test results. But what's in a score?

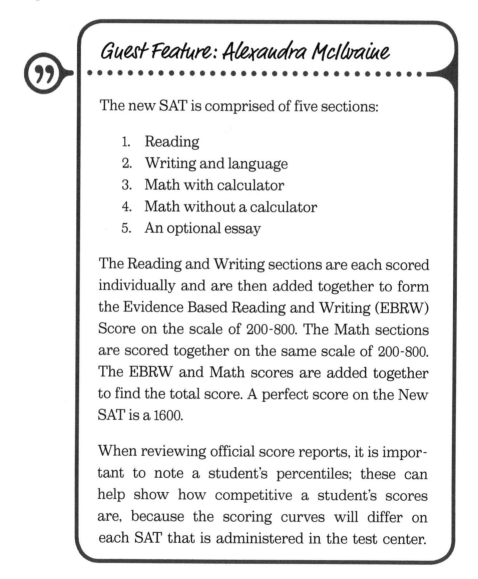

Guest Feature: Alexandra McIlvaine

The new SAT is comprised of five sections:

1. Reading
2. Writing and language
3. Math with calculator
4. Math without a calculator
5. An optional essay

The Reading and Writing sections are each scored individually and are then added together to form the Evidence Based Reading and Writing (EBRW) Score on the scale of 200-800. The Math sections are scored together on the same scale of 200-800. The EBRW and Math scores are added together to find the total score. A perfect score on the New SAT is a 1600.

When reviewing official score reports, it is important to note a student's percentiles; these can help show how competitive a student's scores are, because the scoring curves will differ on each SAT that is administered in the test center.

Hopefully you're not confused at this point — the test has different sections and different pieces that are lumped together, but just know that the three main subjects of the test are reading, writing, and math.

7 Know the Numbers

We've gone over the test pieces, but it's really important that you fully understand the numbers so that you can determine the score you need in order to be accepted into your target schools.

Guest Feature: Clark Steen

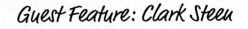

Make sure that you understand the structure of the test and how many questions you need in order to get your target score. Trying to do the entire test is the wrong approach for over 90 percent of students. It makes them rush and get too many easy and medium questions wrong, leading to a low score.

The test is set up so that the easiest questions are first, and the hardest questions are toward the end. If you try to blow through the entire test just to get to the end, you're using the wrong approach. Know how many questions you need to get right in order to hit your target.

Let's take Harvard, for example. Harvard's official site says that there is no specific SAT score required in order to apply: "There are no score cutoffs, and we do not admit 'by the numbers.' For the SAT, we will review your highest test scores in each section across test dates and any other scores you choose to share with us."[1]

That's nice and all, but if you want to be in the ranks with the other applicants, you may want to take a look at the average score of Harvard students in order to see what the school is really looking for. According to PrepScholar, the average college freshman at Harvard earned a 1540 on their SAT (on the new 1600-point scale). PrepScholar goes on to say that while Harvard says there's no score requirement, they really prefer at least a 1480.[2] To put this into perspective, the average SAT score across the country is 1000.

---

1 Harvard College, 2016.
2 PrepScholar, 2016.

So, you want to get a 1480 on the test — how do you know how many questions to answer correctly in order to achieve that?

You take the Evidence-Based Reading and Writing score (up to 800 points) and combine it with the Math score (up to 800 points) to get your total (up to 1600 points). You take the "raw score" of the section you're calculating, which is how many questions you got right, and you convert it into your "scaled score" for that section. Then, you combine the scaled score of both sections to get your total score.

Here's a chart to help you find your scaled score.

Raw Score Conversion Table			
Raw Score (# of correct answers)	Math Section Score	Reading Test Score	Writing and Language Test Score
0	200	100	100
1	200	100	100
2	210	100	100
3	230	110	100
4	240	120	110
5	260	130	120
6	280	140	130
7	290	150	130
8	310	150	140

---

3 CollegeBoard, 2015. The chart has been slightly modified to cut out additional calculations that may cause some to be confused.

Raw Score Conversion Table			
9	320	160	150
10	330	170	160
11	340	170	160
12	360	180	170
13	370	190	180
14	380	190	190
15	390	200	190
16	410	200	200
17	420	210	210
18	430	210	210
19	440	220	220
20	450	220	230
21	460	230	230
21	470	230	230
22	480	240	250
23	480	240	250
24	480	240	250
25	490	250	260
26	500	250	260

Raw Score Conversion Table			
27	510	260	270
28	520	260	280
29	520	270	280
30	530	280	290
31	540	280	300
32	550	290	300
33	560	290	310
34	560	300	320
35	570	300	320

All you have to do is use this conversion chart to find your total score. So, you can achieve the coveted 1480 in a variety of ways. You could get 53/58 on the Math Section, 47/52 on the Reading Section, and 40/44 on the Writing and Language Test. You could also get every question right on the Reading Test as well as the Writing and Language Tests and then miss 10 questions on the Math Section and still get a 1480. As you can see, you can mix and match how well you do on each section, but knowing your strengths is really important so that you can verify how much you need to improve in each section.

8 Know How the SAT Essay Is Scored

The majority of the test is scored by machines, but your essay is scored by a human being. (That kind of rhymed.) Two different people take turns reading and grading your essay. Each person rates your essay on a scale from 1-4 in three different areas: reading, analysis, and writing. Both scores for each of these areas are added together. Then, you'll get three scores for the SAT Essay (one for each area, or dimension) that ranges from 2-8 points.

All of these calculations can be a little hard to follow (skip over this paragraph you math whiz, you), so here's an example. The two scorers — let's name them Thing 1 and Thing 2 — each read your essay. Thing 1 gives you 2 points for reading, 3 points for analysis, and 3 points for writing. Thing 2 gives you 1 point for reading, 4 points for analysis, and 4 points for writing (Thing 2 is a bit extreme, huh?). Add their scores together, and you have your three scores for the SAT Essay — 3 points for reading, 7 points for analysis, and 7 points for writing.

By the way, this may not always be the case due to human error, but the scorers of the SAT Essay are trained to hold every student to the same standards, so in a perfect world, both scorers would probably give you about the same score.

Don't Focus on Controlling Your Score Directly

If you walk into this journey with a number in mind, that's great. Setting goals is always a great idea as it will push you to reach your maximum potential. However, if you sit down to take a practice test and you're trying to control your score directly, you won't have much luck. Focus on pinpointing your flaws and fixing them, and your score will rise as a result.

Guest Feature: Tom Rose

Many new students make the mistake of trying to control their score directly. That's because the score is what matters competitively, and the score is what other people are watching and tracking: friends, parents, and counselors. Here's the problem with focusing on scores: score is an outcome. Trying to control something you don't have any direct influence on is a formula for stress.

Instead, focus on things you *can* control that have shown to improve scores. The most important thing: drive up time spent prepping on a regular basis, and the scores will follow.

10 Report Your Best Score

Gone are the days when you tried to get a perfect score on your first try. Now, you can take the SAT as many times as you need to (in time to report your score to your school of choice). The earlier you start, the better, because you can work toward improving your score and you can then report that winning number on your application. One thing to note, according to the CollegeBoard website, is that you have until nine days after test day to send four free score reports.[4]

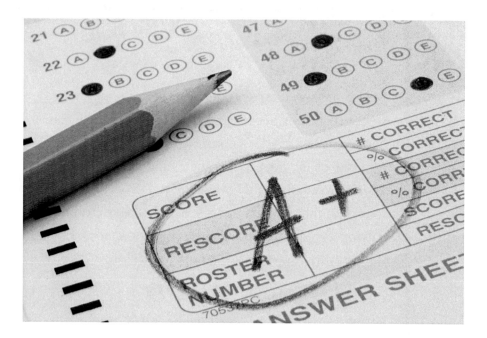

---

4 CollegeBoard, 2016.

Guest Feature: Tom Rose

Starting in 2009, the College Board started a program called Score Choice, triggering a huge strategy change for test-takers. Prior to 2009, students had no choice but to submit the scores for all SAT tests they had taken (or submit none at all). There was no middle ground. That has changed. With Score Choice, students now have the ability to report the scores from only those tests that they choose. This changes strategy dramatically. Under the old system, students would take as few SAT test sittings as possible, because they didn't want to have any low scores on their report to make them look bad. Today, there is no strategic disadvantage to sitting for the test, regardless of how badly you do, because you can simply not report those scores. The dominant strategy now for test taking is to take the test early and keep taking it until you hit your target score.

There are also a few more things to know about score selection.

Some schools have a policy that they call super-score. A super-score is an SAT score built out of your best ever performance on each section. So, you can take your best verbal score ever, and your best math score ever, and put them together to get a "super-score." To use this, obviously you have to at least send those test scores to schools that contain the best-ever performance in a given category so they have the relevant data to create the superscore. (The College Board doesn't allow you to submit scores by section, only entire tests.)

Also, some schools ask that you submit all scores no matter what. If a school asks for all your scores, my recommendation is to report all the scores, because I don't think having some failed efforts on your record makes you look bad. If anything, I think it makes you look gritty and determined. But, if you're really worried about it, you're not required to submit those scores. You can use Score Choice and no one will be the wiser. In other words, use your best judgment.

11 Recognize the New SAT Scoring Flaws

You saw how confusing the scoring of the new SAT can be — that's a pretty big flaw. The older versions of the SAT also gave a penalty for guessing, which helped to keep students from getting perfect scores. Now, the test makers have had to make questions trickier and more advanced to keep scores from being too high across the board. Making questions harder doesn't necessarily help to predict your future college success. If you haven't learned all of this complex stuff, how can you be held accountable for it? The New York Times got a letter to the Editor in February of 2016 titled "Flaws in the New SAT," and writer Bob Schaeffer explains:

"None of the coming changes to the SAT address the test's historic flaws. Some, like increasing the verbal complexity of math problems, may make it worse. [...] Neither the 'new' SAT nor the rival ACT is necessary for high-quality selective admissions. More than 850 accredited, bachelor-degree-granting institutions, including 200 of the most selective in the country, no longer require applicants to submit scores from any standardized exam."[5]

So, while many schools like to see this score on your application, know that like anything else in life — like potato chip bags that are half full of air — the SAT certainly has its flaws.

Guest Feature: Clark Steen

Getting rid of the guessing penalty has caused its own problems. SAT used to rely upon that guessing penalty in order to keep too many students from getting perfect scores and wrecking their bell curve. Because of this, SAT made questions even trickier, added more advanced elements such as trigonometry, and thus attempted to keep scores lower without the unpopular element of the guessing penalty.

---

5 Schaeffer, 2016.

Unfortunately, that had dire consequences. SAT was unsure how this would affect scoring curves, so they ended up never releasing a scoring chart (not even score ranges) in the new SAT book published in July of 2015. They have since released two of the SAT tests that students have taken in April (special administration) and May of 2016. There are score charts for tests, but not enough data for students to reliably predict how many questions they must answer in order to receive their desired score. The scores from March, May, and June of 2016 were so skewed that it took SAT two months to deliver score reports, rather than the two weeks it normally takes.

They are unable to norm their curves, meaning scores are scattered, and it is difficult to put together a scoring scale that even resembles fairness. This also means that colleges do not know how to interpret scores, meaning that the SAT carries even less weight than it did before. Formerly, students needed to get slightly fewer than half the questions correct in order to receive a 500 in a section, which was supposedly the national average. By getting two-thirds of the questions, a student would receive a score of 600 per section, good for most of the competitive schools. Now, College Board needs more information, which is gotten from testing more students. Eventually, they will become much more predictable, but we do not know when that might be. Neither do colleges.

It is a difficult time for schools, as Clark explains, because there are so many different tests to weigh now with different criteria and scoring systems. Alexandra also weighs in on the discussion.

Guest Feature: Alexandra McIlvaine

As far as how colleges consider the redesigned SAT, the test will still be as well respected, if not more so, by admissions officers as it always has been. In reviewing applications, it is simple to compare new SAT students to new SAT students (with respect to standardized test scores), but the trouble comes when you have to compare three students, one of whom has taken the new SAT, one the old SAT and one the ACT— which student do you accept?

CollegeBoard and ACT have created various concordance tables that compare old SAT scores to new SAT scores, as well as tables that compare both old and new SAT scores to ACT scores (view the College Board concordance table here: **https:// collegereadiness.collegeboard.org/educa- tors/highered/scoring-changes/concordance** and the ACT concordance table here: **http://www. act.org/content/dam/act/unsecured/docu- ments/ACTCollegeBoardJointStatement.pdf**). Colleges have had to choose which tables to follow to compare the different scores.

CHAPTER 3

Preparation 101: The Countdown to the Test

I t's the final countdown! I'm hoping a clip from Europe's "The Final Countdown" played in your head. Bad introductions aside, the countdown to the test is here. You need to start studying, you need to register, and you need to find out what to expect. This chapter will ease you through the process.

12 Start Preparing the Summer Before Your Junior Year

You know it's better to start studying early on, but when is the perfect time to begin? Odds are you're going to get all kinds of different advice.

Some will say that you should be mindful of the SAT from the beginning of your high school career. Others will say you can't prepare for it at all. Khan Academy suggests starting SAT prep about three months before your test[1] to give you enough time to try some different study tactics and to really be familiar with the test structure and content.

Guest Feature: Alexandra McIlvaine

We always recommend starting preparation as close to the summer before junior year as possible. We encourage students to complete a diagnostic exam before beginning preparation to assess their strengths and areas of opportunity so we can develop a solid course of action. With the changes to the SAT, there are concepts from higher-level math classes that were not previously part of the test; thus, some students will not have learned all of the necessary concepts at the beginning of their junior year.

Preparing the summer before your junior year is important for two reasons:

1. It is imperative that students have scores locked in before finalizing their college lists so that they understand which schools are truly accessible to them for admission.

---

1 Khan Academy, 2016.

2. Students' grade point averages (GPAs) from their junior year are most important for college applications (since senior year GPAs will not be finalized when college applications are submitted). We have found that finishing standardized testing early on in the junior year reduces the stress students feel and allows them to better focus on their academics to ensure their GPAs fully reflect their academic abilities.

Time is really tricky as you can see — you want to have your scores as early on as possible, but if you haven't taken the classes that teach you the content, you're not going to be as well prepared. Try to find a good balance between SAT prep and managing your current coursework. Don't let your GPA suffer in your junior year as many colleges weigh your high school GPA over your test scores.

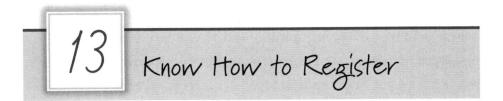

13 Know How to Register

When you are ready to take the plunge, I recommend that you register online and that you take advantage of all the goodies offered during registration. Registering online does require a free College Board account and a credit card. The test fee is $26. A second option is speaking with your school counselors. They should have the paperwork in their office, although mailing or faxing it becomes an extra link in the chain.

Going through a school counselor is the best way to get a fee-waiver form, if you qualify. This form eliminates the fee for taking the SAT. If you say "yes" to any of the following, you are eligible for the fee waiver:

- You're enrolled in or are eligible to participate in the National School Lunch Program (NSLP).
- Your annual family income falls within the Income Eligibility Guidelines set by the USDA Food and Nutrition Service.
- You're enrolled in a federal, state, or local program that aids students from low-income families (e.g., Federal TRIO programs such as Upward Bound).
- Your family receives public assistance.
- You live in federally subsidized public housing or a foster home, or are homeless.
- You are a ward of the state or an orphan.[2]

Your counselor also can help you if you have a learning disability or other needs that might qualify you for special accommodations, such as waiving the time limits on the test. Ask him or her if you think you might need some type of accommodation.

For the most part, online registration is your safest bet. All the information is entered into a computer, which gives you the option to retrieve it later should you lose something. Register at **www.collegeboard.org**.

---

2 CollegeBoard, 2016.

14 Don't Forget About Location

Testing centers are set up in various locales — often in local high schools. When you register, you must designate a first and second location choice. Choosing sites you are familiar with can give you a major advantage.

Eliminating the added stress of testing-center unknowns is another way to take control of that fated Saturday morning and provide a little more peace of mind. This may make room to cram another formula into your brain instead of worries over where you will be testing and how to get there.

If you are forced to choose an unfamiliar center, try to find out something about it. Learn how to get there and how to get in. Check it out if possible; most schools are open after classes. It might feel a little silly, but when you get only five minutes to go to the bathroom, knowing exactly where it is can give you the advantage and the ability to return to the testing room refreshed and relieved without being penalized for time.

That small confidence boost may be just what you need to quell your test butterflies.

15 Start Studying, But Not Too Much

You have your materials, and you're ready to start studying. Maybe you even registered for your test date (go you!). Before you start tackling practice problems, there is one thing you need to be mindful of — studying too much. Wait, what? How can you study too much? Well, first of all, there's such a thing as burnout. This just means that studying too much can exhaust you to the point where studying isn't really doing any good anymore.

Secondly, if you start going through practice problems just to say you went through practice problems, you're not really doing any good. Tom explains the reasoning behind this.

Guest Feature: Tom Rose

Don't churn and burn!

One of the biggest mistakes I see students make is doing way too many practice problems. The mistaken thought process is the following: the more practice questions I do, the higher my score will go. Therefore, I should maximize the number of practice questions I do. Usually, when students follow this format, they start doing what we call "churn-and-burn." They do a ton of practice problems, but learn very little from each one, and consequently their score improvement over time is very low.

This technique does work, it just works very slowly, and soon you'll find yourself running out of practice questions to complete. The activity that I have found to be most closely linked with score improvement is documented learnings: the written list of things that you will do differently in the future. Every time you get a question wrong, you should become a detective and figure out why. Then, figure out what you will do differently in the future so that you don't make the mistake again. Then, *write it down.*

As the list of learnings grows, so will your score. When done properly, I've found that it typically takes three times as long to find and document the learnings as it does to complete the practice questions. So, if you are studying for an hour, you should be doing about 15 minutes of practice questions, and about 45 minutes documenting learnings. If you follow this format, not only will your score improve faster, but you'll also need fewer practice questions to fuel your prep.

16 Bring the Right Supplies

Studying for the exam is definitely a challenge, but here's some good news: bringing the right supplies is extremely easy. Most of the things you might need will not fill up a medium-sized book bag. Here are some basic supplies you'll need to bring to the exam:

- **Bring at least three sharpened #2 pencils, and a couple of dull ones.** If you have a few sharpened pencils, with erasers, you know you will not have to waste precious time sharpening a pencil or waving down a proctor for an eraser. If one breaks, you still have enough leeway for one more to break. I recommend using a dull pencil for bubbling, because it takes less time to fill in the answers.

- **Bring a stopwatch or a watch with a second hand.** Having your own means you can time yourself without worrying about a clock not being in the room. Do not plan to time yourself with a cell phone or other electronic device. They may not be allowed to be out during the test.

- **A calculator is a must.** Make sure you know how to use it before test day, too, and that the batteries are not going to die on you. In fact, to play it safe, bring extra batteries. Do not bring a calculator that prints or makes noises.

- **Bring a bottle of water or some juice.** These fluids are recommended for when you have a break. You also may want to bring a package of crackers or a granola bar for when you get hungry on your break. You will not be able to eat during the test. The test often goes past lunch for most people, and you will start to lose your concentration if you are hungry with no hope in sight. Do not depend on vending machines that may or may not be working. Bring your own drink and snack.

- **Dress in layers so that you will be comfortable.** You do not know what the temperature is going to be like in the testing room, so your best bet is to be prepared for cold, but still give yourself the option of being comfortable if it's too warm. A light or short-sleeved shirt will keep you cool if the room is hot. Bring a sweater or zip-up sweat shirt to put on in case the room is cold. Leave the flip-flops at home and wear shoes with socks. Today is the day to show off your new Js. Or Skechers. Or whatever brand of athletic shoes floats your boat.

You can feel confident that you have the test under control, that you have chosen the right testing center, and that you know what you want out of the SAT, but the suggestions mentioned above are still things you can do to alter your morning and your outcome. Even if you are the kind of person who can enter a timed test without stress or qualms, you can do these things to ensure that you perform to the best of your abilities. This advice may sound cliché, but that's because it *works*.

17 Take the Test From Square 1

Before you even lay your finger on a flashcard, take a practice SAT test. You need to know what you're working with so you can develop your study plan accordingly. You can set up a practice test with a tutor or local SAT prep center. Another option is to take one of the six official full-length practice tests from Khan Academy. Go to **www.khanacademy.org/sat** to sign up and start practicing.

Guest Feature: Tom Rose

I typically suggest that students take the test with no prep as soon as they start thinking about it so that they can get some battlefield experience. Then, with a score in hand, they can look at target schools, compare their performance against their goal, and use that to build a study plan that takes their true score deficit into account. In other words, "Take the test early, with little or no prep, then reassess."

CHAPTER 4

SAT Prep: Plan Your Attack

UH-dum.

DUH-dum.

DUH-dum, DUH-dum, duh-duh, duh-duh, duh-duh, duh-duh, da-da-dum!

Just like battling the world's biggest shark, when taking the SAT, you need to develop your plan of attack. (We all knew that was coming, right?) This chapter will help you do that by determining what your strengths are, how to set goals, and how to fully develop your study plan.

18 Know What You're Good At (And What You Aren't)

Learning your strengths is the key to pinpointing how you'll study for the SAT. But before we figure out what you're good at, perhaps we should consider if you're going to be better suited for the SAT or the sister test, the ACT.

Guest Feature: Alexandra McIlvaine

We always recommend taking an SAT/ACT Diagnostic Test to assess which test is better suited for a particular student. Once a test has been selected by the student, we discuss the student's goals in terms of scores and college acceptances, as well as how much preparation will be necessary to help that student achieve the desired score.

We then review all possible test dates to determine which will work best for the student's schedule. Summer is usually the best time to begin test preparation because students typically have more free time, less stress, and there are four test dates from which to choose in the fall beginning in the 2017-2018 academic year.

If you decide to take a diagnostic test like the one that Alexandra talks about, you'll have a better idea of which way to go. However, if you're already set on taking the SAT, you'll need to decide which areas to focus on.

Hopefully you've taken or have scheduled a time to take a practice test to determine your areas of weakness. This is really the ideal way of finding out how to structure your study plan. Another thing to keep in mind is that you should really examine each section and take away points for any answers you guessed on. One section of the exam might have a slightly inflated score based on guessing rather than your real skill.

19 Make Goals

There's an Instagram post for you — #SATGoals. (Insert eye roll here.) In all seriousness, setting goals is arguably the biggest key to success in virtually every area of life. Once you've determined what your starting point is, you can structure your goals from there.

Let's say you took an SAT practice test, and these were your scores:

Math: 40 questions right (610), Reading: 32 questions right (290), and Writing and Language: 33 questions right (310). Your total score is 1210. Not bad at all, but there's always room for improvement. The best way to pinpoint your goals would be to see what percentage of questions you got right in each section.

Math: 40/58 — 68.9%
Reading: 32/52 — 61.5%
Writing and Language: 33/44 — 75%

As you can see, reading was your lowest score. In this case, you might focus on setting a specific goal of raising your percentage up to, say, 70%. That means your study plan would focus on practicing the reading section a little more than the other sections.

Guest Feature: Clark Steen

Students should aim to take the SAT in the fall of their junior year. This gives them the ability to match scores with schools and determine how much work, if any, needs to be done before the application process. Common wisdom in the past was to take the SAT in the spring of junior year, and if necessary, one more time in the fall. With colleges moving application deadlines up, waiting to take the test is no longer wise.

In addition, students may need to take SAT Subject Tests for more competitive schools. These tests are not always offered on each test date, but when they are, they are offered on the same day as the SAT, making for conflicting schedules. We recommend, if possible, that students have all testing done by June of junior year and to get all applications out the door by September 15th of senior year. This will be sufficient for schools with rolling admissions, as well as being the early bird for early action and early admissions.

My wife and I both worked admissions. You definitely want to get everything done before guidance counselors feel overwhelmed, teachers are sick of recommendations, and admissions officers are so swamped that they want to cry.

20 Create a Study Strategy

Making goals and creating a study strategy really go hand-in-hand. Once you have your goals, you can develop the plan. If you're a very organized person, you might consider purchasing a calendar and writing down which days and for how long you plan to study leading up to the exam. Another option would be to set reminders in your phone. The most important part is that you're intentional about studying — make it a habit. The more immersed in the material you are, the better you will become.

Guest Feature: Clark Steen

Students need to set aside a certain amount of time each week in order to study. The transcript is distinctly more important than standardized testing, which reflects what a student did on one random Saturday morning, but the test still needs a good bit of attention. We recommend that students spend two to three hours per week doing practice problems. As the test looms, we recommend that students do full, timed practice tests, two or more, and do so on a Saturday morning to simulate the real deal.

That said, this book will not be able to rouse you from in front of the television, harangue you to do another practice test, or drill you on grammar rules. If you are one of those students who needs outside motivation to get things done, the structure of a test-prep course might help you immensely. Another option for the motivation-challenged might be to create a study schedule and enlist your parents to enforce it. They have experience with that kind of thing, right? They might even be willing to offer you a reward of some sort for reaching your goal.

In addition, some students may do everything recommended in this book on their own but still feel they need extra help in specific weak areas — algebra, say, or grammar exercises. If that sounds like you, your time and money might be better spent on a few hours of tutoring to work on those areas, instead of on a course that covers the whole test.

Before you do anything beyond what is in this book, check out what resources are available from your school and school district. They may have courses, tutoring, and computerized test-prep programs that are free and readily available.

21 Make Time for the SAT

You have to make time for the SAT if it's really a priority for you. If you're willing to beg your parents to enforce a study rule, the drive and motivation needed for study time is probably already coursing through your arteries. So how much time do you actually need to spend studying in order to see results?

Guest Feature: Tom Rose

There are a million articles written on SAT study strategy, but few written on how to manage SAT prep in your calendar. I have written SAT prep software used by over 100,000 students, and the single biggest predictor of success is time on task. You have to put in the hours. If you're not doing the work, you'll never improve.

At Testive, we typically recommend that students plan to spend a total of 100 hours preparing for the SAT. That includes practice tests and review. The average student using Testive's coaching program spends 50 hours using our software, and 25 hours on real and practice test sittings.

Also, not only do you need to put in about 100 hours total, but how you allocate that time is important. The shorter and more frequent your study sessions, the better. In a best-case scenario, you should be studying six days per week. One of my favorite study plans is an hour-a-day on weekdays and a practice test session each weekend. That'll take you about 10 hours per week, which will allow you to hit your 100 hours in about 10 weeks. Two and a half months is a decent study program. If you haven't hit your goal score after that, a light study program of two hours per week will allow you to keep your edge while you wait for the next test-date to roll around.

As you can see, studying should be a big part of your life during this time, but just remember that the time will pass — the more work you put in now, the better off you'll be in the future.

22 Use Technology to Help You

We live in the digital age, which can be a pain sometimes — my computer just froze… again — but in regards to SAT prep, it can be a huge help.

Guest Feature: Tom Rose

SAT test prep content is getting better and cheaper than it ever has been. New study techniques and adaptive algorithms are lightening the load for students and making each study hour go farther. In particular, there are a few great online resources you can use to prepare that don't cost anything at all.

(1) Khan Academy is a can't-miss resource. Khan has an official partnership with the College Board to release official practice content, and the content is entirely free. The total amount of content on Khan Academy is small, so students will typically be looking for alternate sources to supplement their studies.

(2) One great supplement for Khan is Testive. Testive has over 2000 free practice test questions with video answer explanations, and it was developed by two MIT graduates. As a bonus, Testive's algorithms will keep track of your performance and automatically route you toward content that improves your score the fastest.

(3) Also, a lot can be said for the good old-fashioned paper book. The advantage of the book is that it's a great proxy for the real test, which is also paper-based. Also, a book is very easy to carry around and work on in your idle moments.

Pro-tip: many students rip up their books to save weight, so that they are only carrying around the section they are currently working on. When used properly, you should write ALL OVER your book, so don't worry about reselling it. A pattern I've noticed: the more worn the book, the better-prepared the student.

There are also apps that can help you study. My favorite is an app from The College Board called "Daily Practice for the New SAT®," which offers a practice question every day. You can look through last week's questions along with your answers, and you have access to explanations for every wrong choice. The best part? It's free.

23 | Ask for Help

Don't be afraid to ask for help. Everyone around you is rooting for your success. Tell your friends about your goals, tell your parents that you're prioritizing your studying, and ask the people in your life to keep you on track.

Guest Feature: Tom Rose

With a school test, everyone could score a 90%. In the SAT, exactly 10% of students will score above the 90th percentile. If you want to be one of them, then you need to out-compete the other 90. That means you need to operate at peak performance. Time matters, so efficiency matters. Luckily, this is a time-tested formula for success. If you want to perform at your peak, you must have the following three things:

(1) A goal
(2) A plan
(3) A coach

Your goal is your destination. If you don't know where you're going, you can't get there quickly. Your plan is HOW you'll get there. If you don't have one, you'll meander around and move toward your goal slowly. Your coach is there to keep you on track. If you don't have one, you won't try hard enough.

As a bonus, your coach can also help you set your goal and help you make your plan. They'll also be there with you to celebrate when you succeed!

Many students will say that their parents are not interested in paying for a tutor or prep-program. If you poll parents, as I have, they will almost all tell you that they'd be happy to pay almost any price if their children will happily get off their keister and get serious about prep. Believe it or not, parents feel a tremendous amount of anxiety about test prep, and paying for a tutor is one thing that puts their mind at ease. They are often more interested in shelling out for a tutor than they are in hounding their children to do prep work.

Also, tutors and coaches have a tremendous track record of success when it comes to delivering score improvements. At Testive, students who work with a coach out-improve their self-study peers by a factor of 10. Tutors aren't magical. Here's the big difference: students with coaches do about 10 times as much work, and they are 8 times less likely to quit.

When you're ready to get serious, get a coach.

Chapter **5**

Develop Your Strategies

I don't have a good song for this chapter introduction, but this chapter is still really important. Developing your strategies for the test will no doubt raise your score. Half of the battle is knowing how to be a good test-taker. We will cover timing, answering strategies, and the overall layout of the test.

24 Perfect Your Timing

Timing is everything, especially when the clock is ticking behind you. Tom explains how to best manage your time while actually taking the test.

Guest Feature: Tom Rose

The SAT is long and intense. There is just a little over a minute allocated for answering each question. That will feel like a very quick pace. Because of the intensity of the SAT, there is an athletic component to sitting for the test. You have to manage your intensity and your energy, which means you need to manage your time.

I have taken hundreds of standardized tests, and I now bring a stopwatch with me whenever I do. Don't ever rely on a wall clock or a moderator to time your test. You should also know exactly how much time is allocated for each type of question in a section. Timing on the SAT is so complex that I don't recommend a strict adherence to a linear timing, but rather checking in periodically to make sure that you have crossed certain milestones.

Each SAT section is organized by difficulty, starting with easy questions and ending with hard questions. I usually set a goal of getting to the halfway mark on questions when I'm crossing the one-third mark in time. That means that you'll typically be at a blazing pace for the first half of each section, you'll slow down a bit in the middle, and for the last few minutes of each section, you can reassess your particular situation each time. Count how many questions are left and how much time you have left. Assume that difficult questions will take about double the allowed time for questions in that section. Figure out how many you can squeeze in, then pick the ones that look the best. Guess on the rest.

Don't worry that you feel like you're always running out of time. Everyone feels that way. It's part of the game. I always feel that way, and I've taken the test hundreds of times.

If you get to the point where you are reliably able to answer all the questions in a section, then you are in the 95th percentile of all test-takers. Most people will never get to this point.

Long story short: evaluate your time and assess where you're at while taking the exam. If you're running behind, do your best to pick up the pace.

25 Expect the Directions

If you haven't already done this, sit down and read the directions to every section of the test. That way, you will not have to spend any time reading them when the real test is in front of you. Sure, these directions don't take that long to read, but when every second counts, they can be a huge waste of time. The directions are always the same, as are the sample questions, so reading these self-explanatory paragraphs seems a little unnecessary when you actually take the test.

Guest Feature: Tom Rose

This one is a no-brainer. The directions don't change, and every second counts on the test, so know exactly what you'll be expecting on each section before you get to test day. Wasting a full minute reading directions when you could be answering questions is a big strategic blunder.

26 Underline Key Parts of the Question or Instruction

As you take the test, use your pencil to your advantage. If there is a set of instructions you need to read, underline words and directions that stand out to you as most important. It's like reading a paragraph with a few bolded phrases in it — it immediately draws your attention and makes it much easier to remind yourself what it is that you're supposed to be doing.

27 Know the Layout of the Test

As you may have discovered by now, not all SAT questions are built the same. Most test sections begin with about four to six easy questions to help you ease into the new topic. Then you will get to the bulk of the questions, which are what test-makers consider medium level, or of average difficulty (let's be real, though, they're not all that easy). The last four to six questions are the hardest and the most misleading (insert trick questions here). These aren't exact numbers, but they illustrate a crucial concept: Where you are in the test gives you an idea of how hard a question is meant to be.

28 Let the Easy Questions Be Easy

A lot of the SAT consists of complicated math problems or tricky errors hidden in seemingly perfect sentences. But before you get to those, you will come across a few relatively easy questions. Easy questions often consist of something that's so obvious it seems like it can't be right. "Can it really be this easy?" The answer is, yes, generally, the first few questions in a section can be that easy. For example, say you just started the test and see the following question, which appears to be, well, easy:

Many students often are having trouble making plans and applying to college.

   a) are having
   b) experience having

c) have

d) are

e) is having

In this type of question, the concept being tested is your ability to iden-tify and correct errors in expression of thoughts or, more simply, in the way sentences are structured. In the easy category, this is as simple as reviewing syntax and subject-verb agreement.

Choice *a) are having* is the same as the sentence in the question. In this type of section (identifying errors or the lack thereof), the first answer choice will always repeat what was in the sentence. When you originally read the sentence, a little red flag might pop up in your head. Not only is this an awkward sentence, the verb tense doesn't agree. "Often" signals that this is a continual problem, while "are having" applies only to the current moment. Because you are used to SAT questions being more challenging, you may question this red flag, wondering if this could be a trick question. In the early questions, which are supposed to be easier, don't second-guess your red flag, because the question *can* be that easy.

Just imagine how the sentence should sound. The word "have" fits better in the underlined part of the sentence, and when I look at the answer choices, it's there. I will scan the other answer choices briefly to make sure none of them fit better, but I can choose *c)* without worrying too much about the others.

Guest Feature: Tom Rose

Easy questions are not about getting the answer correct. You are expected to get the answers correct. Easy questions are about speed. You need to answer these at a very fast pace so that you save time for the mind-benders at the end of the section.

Take this information into account when you are practicing. You shouldn't practice easy questions the same way you practice difficult questions. When you practice easy questions, you should do them in blocks of at least five, and you should always be timing yourself. The game is to get them nearly all correct as quickly as possible.

Do drills to lower your time, and keep track of your progress.

Also, when you know you are answering easy questions, you can let your guard down a little bit on trickery. Do you think something feels too easy? That's normal on these questions. You aren't missing anything. Pick an answer and keep moving. Put your guard back up as you start nearing the halfway mark of each section. That's when the deceit starts back up again and you have to be wary of missing tricky details.

29 Watch for the Tricky Middle Questions

A step up from the easy questions, the medium questions might ask for a little more thought or a little more work. Medium questions are more difficult than the easy ones, but at least they don't give you a brain freeze like the trick questions at the end. They are not so easy that they have you second-guessing yourself, but they aren't hard enough to consume all of your time. Knowing the answer you're looking for can cut down on the time you spend on even the medium questions.

Often, math questions will involve an extra step, or sentence completions will have more words you have never seen before in the answer choices. Or (and this is crucial) the question will be nearly as easy as the easy questions, but it includes trick answers to steer you in the wrong direction.

One important strategy in the medium section is not to get tricked. The questions are sometimes fairly simple, but the test-writers prey on the fact that we don't always carefully read and take the time to answer the question on the page. Instead, we answer what we think the question is asking us. Say you encounter the following example about six questions into a math section:

How many right angles are created by the edges of a rectangular cuboid?

> *a) 13*
> *b) 24*
> *c) 45*

d) 57

e) 6

This is a medium question because it expects you to know the vocabulary: *right angles, edges,* and *rectangular cuboid.* These are the key to answering the question. However, finding the correct number involves only that knowledge and not much calculation. You can draw a picture, or you can count the right angles in your head; a right angle on an edge is a corner. Each facet of the cube has four corners and, therefore, four right angles. A rectangular cuboid has six facets. We can decisively say that 6 x 4 = 24 and choose *b)* as the correct answer.

This question should be easy enough to follow, perhaps even easy enough to be an easy question, but the answer choices are meant to trick you, such as *e).* This answer is there because you can jump to the conclusion that a corner is a right angle and then forget to factor in the term "edge." You can answer incorrectly despite the fact that you know the vocabulary and the answer. Since you're getting further into the section, however, you should know to be wary of trick answers and stick with the answer you came up with first.

30 Put Thought Into the Hard Question

By the time you reach the last few questions in a section, you should be extremely wary of a question that seems easy. In the writing section, that means you should think long and hard about whether those red flags that pop up in your brain are steering you to a correct answer or a trick answer. On vocabulary-based questions, you likely will have to try to figure out what unfamiliar words mean.

At this point, any math question that involves a simple concept will require lots and lots of calculation. To prevent unnecessary errors, reviewing is your best weapon on these. If it doesn't involve a lot of calculation, it certainly will require a lot of careful thought and setup. Although you have a calculator to work with, you can't rely on that alone. In fact, many of the harder questions will actually require less calculation but more complex thought.

The following example is a very difficult math question taken from Prep-Scholar's article "The 13 Hardest SAT Math Questions."[1]

If x is the average (arithmetic mean) of m and 9, y is the average of $2m$ and 15, and z is the average of $3m$ and 18, what is the average of x, y, and z in terms of m?

    a) $m + 6$
    b) $m + 7$
    c) $2m + 14$
    d) $3m + 21$

Since the average (arithmetic mean) of 2 numbers is equal to the sum of the 2 numbers divided by 2, the equations $x = (m+9)/2$, $y = (2m+15)/2$, $z = (3m+18)/2$ are true.

The average of x, y, and z is given by $(x+y+z)/3$.

Substituting the expressions in m for each variable (x, y, z) gives $([(m+9)/2+(2m+15)/2+(3m+18)/2])/3$.

---

1 Posted by Courtney Montgomery (2015),
    http://blog.prepscholar.com/hardest-sat-math-questions.

This fraction can be simplified to $m + 7$. The final answer is B.

As you can see, a question like this takes a bit of thought and time. The writer of this post, Courtney Montgomery, explains that if you want a near-perfect SAT score, you should be practicing with questions like this. However, if you're looking to improve an already weak score (let's say you bombed your first practice test and only scored a 200), you should focus on simply raising your overall score instead of delving into the deep end with these very tricky questions.

31 Answer Easy Questions First

This one is self-explanatory, but for the sake of being thorough, move from beginning to end while taking the test. There's no sense in starting out frustrated, so get the easy points as quickly as you can.

Guest Feature: Tom Rose

The questions on the SAT are all worth the same amount, but they are organized from easy to hard. For that reason, you should always answer the sections from front-to-back, just as your instinct would suggest.

In particular, the SAT likes to put a couple of absolutely ridiculous questions in the last three slots of each section. You should be guessing on these unless you have tried every other question in the section already. I will typically go back to questions I have skipped for a second look before I start the last three questions of each section.

32 Master When to Skip or Guess

You don't lose points for guessing on a question, so it's safe to say that you should always be filling in a bubble for every question. However, if you think you might be able to find the answer but you're afraid it may take more time than you want to give just yet, it might be a good idea to skip it and circle back later on.

If you spend too much time trying to figure out a question, you're wasting time you could be using to answer questions you know you can get right. Your limitations are a good thing to have a handle on. When you are taking the test, you should know from a short analysis of a question what your chances are of answering it correctly.

And the only way to know right off the bat if a question is worth skipping or guessing on? Practice. Find your strengths and weaknesses and start learning how long it takes you to answer certain kinds of questions.

33   Keep Track of Where You Skipped or Guessed

It goes without saying that if you decide to skip a question in order to circle back later on, you need to write down what that question is. Nothing is worse than wasting valuable time trying to locate that question you decided to skip. If you end up having extra time even after you've completed the questions you skipped, it can be useful to have a list of questions you totally guessed on so you can check your work.

Let's be honest — you probably won't have the time to do this when all is said and done, but being overly prepared can put you at ease. So, as you make your way through the exam, keep two columns on your spare sheet of paper:

Skipped	Guessed

Keep track of each, and you'll be extra thankful if you end up having a few extra minutes to perfect your score.

34 Practice Good Guessing Skills

Guessing is the perfect tool to use instead of skipping when you see a question you don't want to fully tackle. In that case, you'll want to pick what seems to be the most likely answer choice before you move on.

This strategy is particularly useful in the reading and writing sections where you can use your reasoning skills to rule out a few wrong answers without spending a lot of time on calculations. You'll probably notice that the math section asks you to find the "correct" answer, while the other sections ask you to find the "best" answer. "Best" means you're more often judging among the answer choices to find the one that fits. Often times, you'll look at the answer choices on the hardest reading and writing questions and think, "Well, none of these seem quite right, but those ones are definitely not it."

The rules for guessing are simple. First, you don't want to guess if every answer choice looks like an equally decent choice to you. This is random guessing, and the SAT is designed to punish it. If you can eliminate a few options, that's called educated guessing, which is worthwhile. Any time you can spend narrowing down the number of answer choices you are deciding amongst is time well spent, because you're increasing your odds of earning one more point — and making up for four wrong answers. If you're picking between two answer choices on the most difficult reading questions, you're likely to do quite well on that section.

Good guessing is all about eliminating wrong answers to find what might be the right one. Let's delve into the next tip, which will fully explain the process of elimination.

35 Use the Process of Elimination

If the answer doesn't sucker punch you in the face right away, use the process of elimination. Expert Tom Rose will explain this strategy a bit more, but let's first use an example to get a breakdown of this important strategy.

Without certain knowledge, some people have a(n) _____ that can cause problems when they are trying to succeed in a specific field.

    a) viscosity
    b) prejudice
    c) deception
    d) injury
    e) surplus

Beginning this question, you might try to fill in the blank. It has so many possible answers that all you can conclude is the blank carries a negative connotation. This is apparent because the "people" are "without certain knowledge" and it "can cause problems." These context clues allow you to decide that the blank is the source of the problem and, therefore, a bad thing or a word with a negative connotation.

With this information, all you can eliminate is *e) surplus* because "people" who have a surplus would have a bounty of information. This does not connect with the assertion that the missing word is negative. At this point, you should scan the rest of the answer choices. The options that are left include three words with a negative connotation and one word, *viscosity*, which you might not know. Here is a time to stop and take stock of where you stand. If you do know the meaning of *viscosity*, pretend you don't and stick with me.

I would expect the word in the blank to indicate a lack of knowledge, like another word for *ignorance*, but none of the answer choices seems to reflect that idea. If none of the answer choices seems great, and you have no idea what *a) viscosity* means, you have two options. You can omit the question. It won't cost you anything, and you can move on without wasting time or sweating over it. However, you have already omitted one answer choice, so it's a better idea to guess. Before just picking one of the other four answers, let's see if we can eliminate some others.

You don't want to eliminate *a) viscosity* just because you don't know what it means. Looking at this sentence, you should be able to tell that *a) viscosity* is a noun and theoretically would fit into the structure, so you can't eliminate it for that reason either. You can skip over it for now, however, and try to determine which of the other answers could fit better.

Our first option is *b) prejudice*. Since the sentence is ambiguous and you don't know the field, you can substitute *prejudice* for the blank and the sentence continues to flow:

> *Without certain knowledge, some people have a <u>prejudice</u> that can*
> *cause problems when they are trying to succeed in a specific field.*

This word fits, because it satisfies the conditions set forth in the problem. If someone holds a prejudice, he or she may be uneducated about something. This, in turn, can cause a hindrance. The sentence advocates this, but since you have other words that fit the negative category, and you are looking for the b*est* answer choice, you also must examine the other choices.

Moving on to *c) deception*, you can follow the same strategy. With this answer choice, the sentence would read:

> *Without certain knowledge, some people have a <u>deception</u> that can*
> *cause problems when they are trying to succeed in a specific field.*

Although *deception* is also a noun, the sentence sounds awkward and doesn't make much sense. People can fall subject to a deception, but rarely will you find it worded that someone *has* a deception.

Eliminating *c)*, you can proceed to *d) injury* and explore this last option. Plug in *injury* into the blank and see if it also works:

> *Without certain knowledge, some people have an <u>injury</u> that can*
> *cause problems when they are trying to succeed in a specific field.*

This word is also a negative noun, and it even fits within the sentence structure. The catch with this answer choice is that having an injury in the traditional sense does not have much to do with knowing certain information. Not knowing information could end up causing you harm, but this is not a direct cause, and the sentence calls for a direct cause. The injury could be metaphorical, but since you are looking for the *best* answer choice, the rule is you should not have to stretch the answer to make it fit.

Go back to the first answer choice. First, plug it into the sentence to see how it sounds. This is a vital skill when trying to determine whether a word fits. In this scenario, it is difficult to discover the meaning of the word by plugging it in. You might reason that *viscosity* is unlikely to be a synonym for *ignorance*, which is what you are really hoping to find. Not knowing what *viscosity* means, you now have a situation where you could guess. Since you have narrowed your chances of getting what you believe to be the correct answer from one out of five to one out of two, you should guess between those two answer choices.

So is your choice *a)* or *b)*?

Viscosity refers to the fluidity of a liquid and a resistance to flow. In this sentence, the blank word references the person's inability to change. This does apply in the situation, but in this case, it's not the best fit. *Prejudice* makes the sentence more coherent and is the correct answer.

Questions such as these often require some elimination followed by an educated guess between the remaining choices.

Guest Feature: Tom Rose

Math questions have a 'right' answer that you solve for and then pick from the list of options. Verbal questions, on the other hand, require judgment. The correct answer isn't always absolutely correct. A better way to describe the correct answer in the verbal section is to say that the correct answer is the "best" answer. The "best" answer isn't something that can be picked on its own, but rather must be chosen from among a set and judged against other options in the set. For that reason, you should always be using a process of elimination for all verbal questions. That is, rather than picking the right answer, you should be eliminating three wrong answers and picking whatever is left.

Many students are resistant to this technique at first, because they feel like it takes longer, and they're right. It does take longer, at first. Fortunately, you'll get better over time, and having a process will actually make you faster once you learn how to use it.

Unfortunately, process of elimination is the only reliable way to repeatedly pick correct answers on the verbal section of the SAT. Remember, the objective of the test-writer (I was a test-writer for many years) is to develop answer choices that trick the test-taker into picking them. The industry term for incorrect answer choices is actually "distractors."

Distractors are specifically there to try to distract, or fool the test-taker into picking them. Since verbal questions require judgment, your only reliable defense against distractors is to use a process of elimination. Start doing it now, even though it's painful. Eventually, it will get easier, and eventually, you'll be a lean, mean, elimination-machine.

36 Find the Answer You're Looking For

The SAT's multiple-choice format offers many opportunities to fall into traps, because it has answer choices in every section that are written deliberately to trick you. Don't worry, though — these questions won't be a problem for you, because you're a rockstar, and you're going to use a really important strategy. Whenever possible, you're going to know the answer before you even look at the answer choices.

In other words, you'll answer questions by deciding among the answer choices only as a last resort. Instead, you're going to answer questions by choosing the answer choice that matches, or is closest to, *your* answer.

Ignoring that the SAT is a multiple-choice test, you can decide what you think the answer is and find the one that matches. In the math section, if you did the problem correctly, your answer should be there. If it isn't, re-evaluate your work. In the reading and writing sections, your exact answer may not show up, but you will choose the answer choice that most closely resembles your answer whenever possible.

Here is a sample question illustrating this snare that traps many test-takers:

The diagram below represents a 120-square-foot plot of land that is 15 feet long from east to west. How long is the side of the plot that goes north-south? (Note: drawing not to scale)

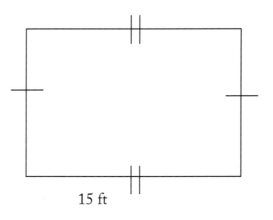

15 ft

a) 8 ft
b) 15 ft
c) 45 ft
d) 75 ft
e) 105 ft

If, upon seeing this question, you are a little confused by it, you might look at the answer choices for guidance. Our example question highlights the pitfalls of this method, because the answers are designed to trick you. As you seek guidance, you might notice that answer choice *b) 15 ft* would make this figure a square. From there, you might see that the question mentions "square feet." It also says it isn't drawn to scale, so it could be a square even though it looks like a rectangle.

Similarly, the marks showing that the opposite sides are the same length do not rule out the possibility that all four sides are the same length. Bingo! You have the answer. The other side has a length of 15, because this is actually a square. Wrong. "Square feet" is a unit of measure that applies to the area of a square or a rectangle. When you calculate the area, you have taken two sides in "feet" and multiplied them together, effectively squaring the unit "feet" and making it "square feet."

You also might look at *c) 45*, and notice that if one side were this length, then the opposite side also would have a length of 45. Since the side opposite the 15-foot side also would have a length of 15, you could add them all together: 15+15+45+45=120. But in this scenario, 120 would be the perimeter of the figure, not the area, which is what you are given in the question. This is a common mistake among test-takers who scan the answer choices first. They see an answer that fits a concept they know and, in a rush, they choose it. Perimeter and area are often confused, so the test-makers take advantage of that to create trick answers.

If you were in a real rush, you also might be tempted by *e) 105*, which is what you would get if you subtracted the length of one side, 15, from the area, 120. Finally, if you are trying to eliminate wrong answers, you may notice that all of the answer choices are multiples of "5," except for *a) 8*. This might lead you to believe that *a)* is not the answer because it does not fit the pattern.

You would be wrong, because *a)* is the answer. To arrive at the answer, you only need to slightly manipulate the two numbers given. To find the area, you multiply the length and width, and you know that the area is 120. Therefore, you might write the equation: $15x = 120$. Then you would divide both sides by 15 and find that $x = 8$. Once you do that, you will see that this is one of the answer choices, and you choose it without a second thought.

If this is the method you use, you can be sure that the test's tricks will not ensnare you. On a question such as this, scanning the answer choices first is also a waste of time that would be better spent just working through the problem.

37 ...Or Know How to Find the Answer

The opposite way to approach the test is to look at the answers before you figure out the question. At the risk of contradicting myself, I suggest that this method also can be helpful. Let me explain. For every multiple-choice question, your best bet is coming up with an answer before you ever look at the answer choices. Ideally, you will form an answer in your brain, then find it among the choices. On math questions, this means solving the problem and choosing an answer. For reading and writing, it means looking for the answer that most closely fits your prediction. This is the best way, because you are less likely to be distracted by wrong answer choices. You also can save time and save yourself the stress of second-guessing. If you know the answer and you are pretty confident, just pick it and move on.

This strategy does not work on every question, though, because some questions are simply not within reach. To put it bluntly, this method doesn't work if you are totally clueless. If you can't seem to come up with a prediction or have no idea what the question is looking for, your only option is to scan the answer choices to get on the right track. Checking the answer choices sometimes can help you find enough direction to work out a problem on your own. On math questions, this might mean looking to see what type of answer you need, such as a fraction or a variable. Then, you can try again to set it up.

On vocabulary questions, scanning the answer choices might help you figure out whether you are looking for a single word or a phrase. Then, you can come up with a prediction. If you are still clueless, see if you can eliminate a few answer choices and guess. If nothing else works, the answer-choice strategy might be to look for the best option given. Take this question from the writing section, for instance:

The two teams could not decide on the tree as a better base or, on the other hand, to leave the bridge as the base.

> a) *the tree as a better base or, on the other hand, to leave the bridge*
> b) *the tree as a better base or them keeping the bridge*
> c) *the tree making a better base or them keeping the bridge*
> d) *the tree as a better base or leaving the bridge*
> e) *the tree as making a better base and leaving the bridge*

There are some tricky elements to this problem, even though it is just a medium-difficulty question. When you get down to what it's looking for, the question asks whether you can settle on verb agreement in a more complex context. First, you should try to decide on what might be a good fix to the underlined part. But try as you might, no solution comes. Or even more likely, there are so many ways to fix this problem that you aren't really sure where to start.

So, you try your second-choice tactic and just read the answer choices. You will find that you can eliminate *c)* and *e)* pretty easily because the verb "making" doesn't sound right; it doesn't add to the structure of the sentence. You also want the sentence to be expressed clearly and concisely, and the extra words in those choices muddle the meaning. You can eliminate b) — not grammatically correct because of "them keeping" — which leaves us with *a)* and *d)*. The first option, choice *a)*, is the original sentence, and the second, *d)*, changes the sentence tense from "leave" to "leaving" while eliminating the extraneous phrase "on the other hand."

The answer in this case is *d)*, because it clears up and denotes exactly what the two teams were struggling with in their decision, the tree versus the bridge. You might not have come up with that answer on your own, but you found it by using the process of elimination. Even if you ended up choosing *a)*, you had a 50-50 chance of choosing the right answer, because you had eliminated three wrong answer choices. If you do this consistently, your score will improve overall.

38 Study Your Mistakes

It's really important to focus on learning why you got an answer wrong in order to improve your overall score. Studying your mistakes is proven to be more effective than doing practice problem after practice problem.

In order to maximize your time, you should first know what your best learning style is.

Guest Feature: Alexandra McIlvaine

The three most basic learning styles are auditory, visual, and kinesthetic. An auditory learner learns best by hearing, a visual learner learns best by seeing, and a kinesthetic learner learns best by doing. At Educational Services, we work with students with a wide range of academic abilities from a 1.0

GPA to a 4.0 GPA, and we work with students who take the test in regular time as well as those who have testing accommodations of time and a half, double time, triple time, readers, and more. With such a varying group of students, there are those that combine multiple learning styles and those that fall outside the three common learning styles, because they process information differently.

Once you can pinpoint what your most effective learning style is, you can learn how to attack questions. Which do you prefer? A lecture, a PowerPoint presentation, or hands-on task? Then you can cater your study time to make sure you're making the most of it.

Guest Feature: Tom Rose

One of the things we spend lots of time explaining to students at Testive is that they should spend three minutes "reviewing" for every one minute "doing." What we're getting at with that advice is that students should spend three times as long studying their mistakes as they do answering questions in the first place. Reviewing mistakes properly is very time consuming, but very valuable. It is arguably the most useful allocation of study time.

At Testive, for every question that students answer incorrectly, we require that they write an explanation, in their own words, of what they will do differently next time they face a similar situation. We call these 'review notes'. My belief is that the documenting of review notes is the single most important feature of our learning program, and the data bears that out. Students who write good review notes out-improve their non-noting peers by 3-to-1. That is, for each non-reviewer improving their score by 100 points, there is a reviewer improving their score by 300 points. And this is true for students who spend the same amount of time studying.

What our data shows is that if you have one hour to spend doing prep, you're better off doing 15 questions and spending 45 minutes reviewing your mistakes and writing review notes than you are answering 60 questions.

39 Bubble at the End

While some of the tactics we cover will be harder to master, this one is a no-brainer — save time by bubbling all your answers at the end.

Guest Feature: Clark Steen

Make sure to bring some sharp and dull #2 pencils. Sharp pencils are good for writing. Dull pencils are great for bubbling. Do not bubble any answers until close to the end of the section. Studies (by the College Board) have shown that bubbling all at once reduces errors to virtually zero and saves the student significant time on each section.

CHAPTER 6

Math Strategies: Winning the Numbers Game

Some people are natural mathematicians. Ask them what 50 x 12 is, and out comes 600. There are also those of us that still use our fingers to do basic addition — cough, me included — but no matter what your skill sets are, you will need to spend time studying and honing in on the math section of the SAT. This chapter will go over some simpler strategies as well as more complex ones to make sure you're fully aware and capable of getting your ideal score in this daunting section.

40 Get the Right Calculator and Prep It Correctly

Not only are there tons of calculator brands to choose from, but each brand has a slew of different models. To help narrow down your search slightly, here is a list of calculators that are approved for use on the SAT, sorted by brand [1]:

Casio:

- FX-6000 series
- FX-6200 series
- FX-6300 series

---

1 As of January 2017 from **https://collegereadiness.collegeboard.org/sat/ taking-the-test/calculator-policy**.

- FX-6500 series
- FX-7000 series
- FX-7300 series
- FX-7400 series
- FX-7500 series
- FX-7700 series
- FX-7800 series
- FX-8000 series
- FX-8500 series
- FX-8700 series
- FX-8800 series
- FX-9700 series
- FX-9750 series
- FX-9860 series
- CFX-9800 series
- CFX-9850 series
- CFX-9950 series
- CFX-9970 series
- FX 1.0 series
- Algebra FX 2.0 series
- FX-CG-10 (PRIZM)
- FX-CG-20

Hewlett-Packard:

- HP-9G
- HP-28 series
- HP-38G
- HP-39 series
- HP-40 series
- HP-48 series

- HP-49 series
- HP-50 series
- HP Prime

Radio Shack:

- EC-4033
- EC-4034
- EC-4037

Sharp:

- EL-5200
- EL-9200 series
- EL-9300 series
- EL-9600 series*
- EL-9900 series

*You cannot use the stylus.

Texas Instruments:

- TI-73
- TI-80
- TI-81
- TI-82
- TI-83/TI-83 Plus
- TI-83 Plus Silver
- TI-84 Plus
- TI-84 Plus CE
- TI-84 Plus Silver
- TI-84 Plus C Silver
- TI-85
- TI-86

- TI-89
- TI-89 Titanium
- TI-Nspire/TI-Nspire CX
- TI-Nspire CAS/TI-Nspire CX CAS
- TI-Nspire CM-C/TI-Nspire CM-C CAS
- TI-Nspire CX-C CAS

Other Calculators:

- Datexx DS-883
- Micronta
- Smart2

According to our featured guest Clark Steen, the calculator to have is the Texas Instruments TI84 graphing calculator. So, that was easy, right?

Wait — there's more! Steen advises you to pre-program your calculator with the math formulas you're going to need for section 4 of the SAT. He explains how.

Guest Feature: Clark Steen

Push Prgm, then New, then name the program SAT Math. Add all of the formulas by pushing the Alpha key to get to the letters above each key on the calculator. Press 2nd Mode (Quit) to exit. If you push Clear, you will start wiping out some of the lines of text you entered.

To access the formulas during the test, just push Prgm, then Edit, then SAT Math. Write down whatever formula you need. Voila! You have a perfectly legal math cheat sheet on your calculator.

*Quick Note: If you change batteries on your calculator, take out only one battery at a time and replace it with one new battery. If you take out all four batteries at once, you can lose your programs. Wouldn't want that!

41 Use Your Calculator Sparingly

Your calculator should only be used when necessary. When you work problems out on paper, you're giving your brain the advantage of having a visual to work from. We humans generally respond well to visuals.

Guest Feature: Clark Steen

Make everything visual. Draw and label everything. Don't do anything in the calculator until you have written it down. Fifty percent of the average human brain is dedicated to seeing things and interpreting what has been seen. Make everything visual to feed the brain information the way it likes to be fed.

42 Know the Formulas Given to You

Formulas are tough, but the more time you spend committing them to memory, the better off you'll be come test time. Here are some basic formulas you should definitely know before walking into the room.

Area of a Circle: $A=\pi r^2$

Circumference of a Circle: $C = 2\pi r$

Area of a Rectangle: $A = lw$

Area of a Triangle: $A = \frac{1}{2} bh$

The Pythagorean Theorem: $a^2+b^2=c^2$

Guest Feature: Alexandra McIlvaine

We always recommend making flashcards or using Quizlet, a learning website (and app!), to help memorize all of the necessary formulas. Although some of the basic formulas are given to you in the front of each section, there are a lot of formulas that are not given. The New SAT's math sections have more advanced concepts than the previous version of the SAT, and so the formulas provided in the test do not cover all need-to-know formulas including those corresponding to the unit circle and radians.

Unit Circle:

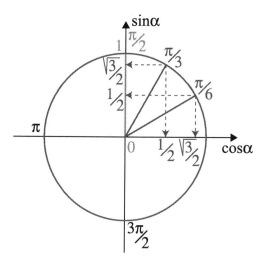

Sine Function: **sin(θ) = Opposite / Hypotenuse**
Cosine Function: **cos(θ) = Adjacent / Hypotenuse**
Tangent Function: **tan(θ) = Opposite / Adjacent**

Cofunction Identities, radians:

$\sin(\pi/2 - X) = \cos x$ $\qquad$ $\cos(\pi/2 - X) = \sin x$

$\tan(\pi/2 - X) = \cot x$ $\qquad$ $\cot(\pi/2 - X) = \tan x$

$\sec(\pi/2 - X) = \csc x$ $\qquad$ $\csc(\pi/2 - X) = \sec x$

Cofunction Identities, degrees:

$\sin(90° - x) = \cos x$ $\qquad$ $\cos(90° - x) = \sin x$

$\tan(90° - x) = \cot x$ $\qquad$ $\cot(90° - x) = \tan x$

$\sec(90° - x) = \csc x$ $\qquad$ $\csc(90° - x) = \sec x$

43 Write Other Formulas Down First

No matter how much information you cram into your brain, sometimes you just can't remember it all. This is particularly true when SAT pressure is bearing down on you. Under that level of stress, things you think you know can escape you. However, you do have ways to avoid this, particularly when it comes to the formulas that the SAT doesn't provide.

Anything that you're not sure you will remember, including formulas in the math section, you should write down as soon as you start. When it comes time to use the formula, you may draw a blank. But if you've already written it down, you can just flip back a page or two and save yourself the agony of banging your head on the desk trying to remember.

To maximize this strategy, create a list of formulas that you know you'll need on the test as you study. Don't worry about including formulas that you know by heart. Also, don't worry about formulas that the test will give you.

Once you have a list, knowing it by heart should be part of your study plan. Unlike most of the ways you study, this will involve straight memorization. Once you think you have them, practice sitting down cold and writing them all at once. Be sure you practice this as test day comes closer so that you don't forget them.

It's also a very good idea to rewrite the formula on every section, because you are not allowed to view previous test sections after time is called. You don't want the proctor to ask you to leave and then end up with a voided score because you flipped to the prior section where you wrote your formulas.

44 When In Doubt, Try 1, 2, or 7

Sometimes, you try and try (and try) and just can't crack the code. If you have absolutely no clue what number to write down for an open-ended question, try writing down the number 1, 2, or 7.

Guest Feature: Alexandra McIlvaine

They use numbers 1, 2, and 7 a lot. However, if they say it's a four-digit number that is even, obviously try to take an educated guess. The chance is small that a student will get it correct, but we have seen it happen.

This is obviously a last resort guessing tip, but hey — sometimes you have to give it your best shot in the dark!

45 Use the Answer Choices to Your Advantage

Ideally, you want to be able to solve every math problem yourself, then just look for the answer that matches yours. It also pays to double-check your answers. Sometimes, however, you will have no idea how to solve a problem. Other times, you will suspect that getting to the right answer is going to take an excessive amount of time. In either case, one good option is to try looking at the answer choices.

Guest Feature: Clark Steen

All but 14 of the SAT Math questions have answers. Using the answer choices is critical to doing well. When there are variables in the answers, students should substitute their own real numbers for variables, then put those real numbers into the answers to see which one matches. This is like coming up with a formula, and then putting in test values to check the accuracy of the formula, except that there are five formulas in the answers.

If there are only real numbers in the answers, students should take the answers and try to put them back in for a value or variable or measurement and simply see if it works. I always start with answer choice C. If C is incorrect, you will know to go up or down to start eliminating the other options.

46 Master Math Vocabulary

It's true — vocabulary isn't just for the critical-reading section. A few math questions will test you on knowing terms such as *integer* and *mean*. Even more questions will test other, more advanced concepts but will still be impossible to answer without knowing exactly what every word in the question means. To familiarize you with some of the many math terms you will see on the SAT, here is a quiz for you to take. Try to answer all the questions before peeking ahead at the answers.

- *What are the first five prime numbers?*
- *Which of the following is not an integer [-1, 0, ½, 1]?*
- *In the number set [2, 2, 4, 5, 7], what are the mean, median, mode, and range?*
- *Is the number set [2, 4, 6, 8, 10] made up of consecutive integers?*
- *What is the difference between a number and a digit?*

Some of these terms should be pretty familiar, while others you may have learned so long ago that cobwebs have formed around that section of your brain. Here are the answers, which contain crucial knowledge for the math section:

1. A prime number is a natural number that is greater than 1 and is divisible only by itself and 1. Therefore, the first five prime numbers are 2, 3, 5, 7, and 11. Note that 1 is not a prime number, while 2 is the only even prime number.

2. An integer is any whole number, whether positive or negative. Fractions, however, are not integers, so the answer is ½.

3. Mean is another word for average, which in this case is 4. You would find the average by performing the following: (2 + 2 + 4 + 5 + 7)/ 5 = 20 / 5 = 4. We will discuss the formula for average in the next tip. The median is the number that is in the middle of the set when it is ordered numerically. This set is in numerical order, so the median is 4. The mode is the number that occurs most, in this case 2. The range is the difference between the largest and the smallest number, in this case 7 − 2 = 5.

4. No. This would be considered a sequence of numbers because they follow a set pattern. Consecutive integers, however, must follow one right after another, such as [1, 2, 3, 4, 5].

5. Let us look at an example here: 4,346,980. This is only one number, even if it is a rather long one. It includes seven digits, however.

47   Know Your Averages

You use a few formulas in daily life without giving them much thought, but the way they show up on the SAT makes it worthwhile to consider them more carefully. The first of these is averages. Say your grades on English tests this semester were 97, 94, and 98. You weren't even bothering to average these, because you were doing so well. Then, you took another test and got a 67. Most students would wonder how badly their overall grade was damaged. To do that, you would take an average:

$$(97 + 94 + 98 + 67) / 4 = 356 / 4 = 89.$$

You realize now that you will have to work a bit to get your A average back, but you probably didn't think much about the formula you used, which looks like this:

Average = (Sum of the values in the series) / (Number of items in the series).

48   Calculate Percentages Like a Pro

Another formula that you may use without thinking of it is percentages. For instance, if you see that a particular pair of shoes you want is usually

$89 but they're on sale for 35 percent off, you probably would get right to it to see if you could afford them: 89 x .35 = 31.15

So, to find the discount, you used a formula that could be written like this: Whole x Percent = Part.

You also made an important adjustment that you may not have considered. When you have a percentage but need to convert it to a number so that you can calculate, you must divide by 100. So, 35% / 100 = .35. One way to think about it is that you must divide by 100 to take away the percentage symbol (%).

Next, you would subtract that discount from the original total, making your new cost 89 – 31.15 = $57.85.

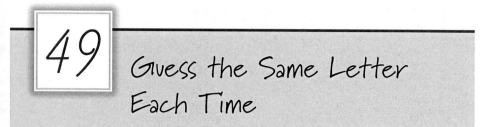

49 Guess the Same Letter Each Time

Similar to guessing 1, 2, or 7 is bubbling in the same letter every time you take a wild guess. Play the probably odds by choosing the same letter instead of alternating between guesses. Your odds of landing a correct guess will go up.

> ### Guest Feature: Clark Steen
>
> Any questions you do not answer, just guess the same letter each time. The letters are equally distributed between A, B, C, and D, so if you guess the same letter each time, you can get a predictable one-fourth of the questions correct.

50 Follow the 30-Second Rule

Math questions can be misleading. You may begin one thinking "Yeah, I feel pretty good about this one!" Then, before you know it, you've dedicated five minutes to a problem that's leading you down a deep, dark rabbit hole with no confident answer in sight. A good rule of thumb is to follow what Clark Steen calls "the 30-second rule."

Guest Feature: Clark Steen

If you get more than 30 seconds into a problem and have no idea what you are doing, cut bait and move on. Don't "grudge" a problem. They are all worth one point. Go to another problem.

51 Avoid Mental Math

Even if you're a genius and smirk when you see others counting on their fingers, you should avoid mental math. You're much more likely to catch a silly (or not so silly) mistake if you can trace back to where the issue is. When you practice for the math section, make sure to take the time to write out the entire order of operations on paper.

Guest Feature: Alexandra McIlvaine

We advise our students to avoid mental math and to put all their work directly on the test booklet. It was a challenge for many students when the non-calculator section of the test was added since students generally have access to calculators in school. The act of writing down the steps for each problem will not only help students who are visual learners to see their mistakes, but it will also help other students to see the next logical step.

52 Don't Always Solve for X

While algebra classes often focus on finding a concrete answer for a particular variable, the SAT often asks for some variation on that theme.

Because the questions are set up differently, you must stop yourself from diving in by doing what comes naturally: solving for x. Instead, you must carefully examine what the question is asking you to find before you start solving. Consider the following problem.

If $2(x + y) - 2 = 14$, then $x + y$ equals:

- *5*
- *6*
- *7*
- *8*
- *9*

A diligent algebra student might see the equation and start solving for x, which would look something like this:

$2(x + y) - 2 = 14$
$2x + 2y - 2 = 14$
$2x = 16 - 2y$
$x = (16 - 2y) / 2$

So, you solved for x, but that is not what you were asked to do. Instead, you were asked to solve for what is inside the parentheses, x + y, which is actually easier:

$2(x + y) - 2 = 14$
$2(x + y) = 16$
$(x + y) = 8$
So you would choose answer choice *d)*.

Even an easy question can be tricky or time-consuming if you do not read it carefully enough and start working it the wrong way. You can waste time trying to figure out x or y when you do not need to. By carefully reading the questions — all of them, not just the ones that are long and intimidating — you can help yourself out by avoiding wasted time.

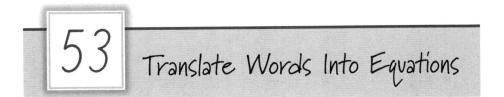

53 Translate Words Into Equations

A good number of the math questions on the SAT are what you might call "word problems." In fact, so many of them are word problems that this name is almost meaningless. Word problems can test all kinds of concepts, from number properties to geometry, so you cannot treat them as a group and approach them with a single strategy.

One skill is extremely useful in word problems. We will call it translation: taking the words in the problem and translating them into equations using numbers and variables. This skill is particularly important when the question is written out in words but the answer choices are riddled with x's and y's. In that case, you are facing a translation problem. A good approach to these problems is to go word by word, translating words to symbols. Here are a few key translations:

    a) "Is" means "="
    b) "And" means "+"
    c) "Less than" or "fewer" means "−"
    d) "Double" means "x 2"

The list can go on and on, but the truth is you know these translations. You just never thought about them. As you take SAT practice tests, however, you *do* need to think about them. Try this translation problem to see how it works:

> *On a family vacation, Mom drove m miles, while Dad drove twice as many miles as Mom, and Susan drove 40 miles fewer than Dad. How many miles did Susan drive, in terms of m?*
>
> *a) 2m + 40*
> *b) 2m − 40*
> *c) m / 2 + 20*
> *d) (m + 20) / 2*
> *e) m / 2 − 20*

You may have noticed I tricked you a little because this question uses terms that are different than the ones I have listed above yet mean the same things: "double" means the same thing as "twice as many," and "fewer" means the same thing as "less than." I did this to bring up an important point. Much like the English language overall, SAT math questions have many ways to express one idea. Practicing translation, then, is not an exercise in memorization. It takes practice breaking down words one by one. We will do that with our example:

We start with the variables:

> a) m = number of miles Mom drove
> b) d = number of miles Dad drove
> c) s = number of miles Susan drove

Now put them in the right order. Dad drove twice as many miles as Mom. Therefore: d = 2m (You would have to double Mom's miles to reach Dad's miles, in other words.)

Susan drove 40 miles fewer than Dad, so: s = d – 40 (If you took 40 miles from Dad's total, you would have Susan's total.)

How do we put these together to form an equation representing "s" (Susan's miles) with only the variable "m"? We can start with Susan's equation and replace the "d" with "2m," using the information from our first equation, d = 2m.

> s = d – 40
> s = 2m – 40

The correct answer is *b) 2m – 40.*

Note that this problem involved no calculation, only logic and translation. Many word problems are like this, making translation a crucial way to earn points quickly.

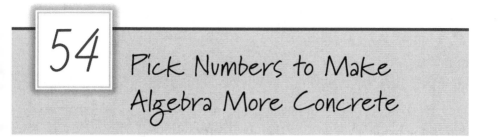

One way to tame an unruly set of x's and y's is to replace them with real numbers. This works particularly well when the question tells you something about what x and y should be. Take this question for instance:

If x is an even integer and y is an odd integer, which of the following would be an odd integer?

- *3x*
- *y + 3*
- *2y + x*
- *y + 2x*
- *4y*

The correct answer choice here will be true for all even and odd integers, so the easiest way to solve it will be to pick an even and an odd number to stand for x and y, then try the answer choices. Say that:

$$x = 2$$
$$y = 3$$

Plug these into the answer choices and see which one produces an odd number:

- $3 (2) = 6$
- $3 + 3 = 6$
- $2(3) + 2 = 8$

- $3 + 2(2) = 7$
- $4(3) = 12$

Answer choice *d)* is the only one that turns out to be odd, so this is the correct answer.

Look for chances to replace variables with numbers throughout the test. It can save you time or even help you get the right answer when you might not have otherwise.

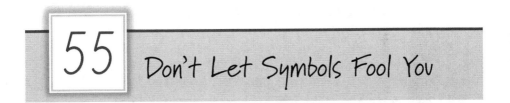

55 Don't Let Symbols Fool You

Even worse than an overflow of x's and y's are the made-up symbols included in some questions. These could be happy faces, exclamation points, or anything else the test-makers can come up with to confuse you.

These symbols intimidate many a test-taker, because they're unfamiliar. However, most of the questions using symbols ask you to do little more than plug numbers or variables into the equation the symbol represents.

We will break down one of these questions to get you comfortable with how they work:

For all numbers a and b, let a @ b be defined as a @ b = a / b + (a − b).
What is the value of (10 @ 5) @ 2?

a) 5
b) 8.5
c) 10
d) 12.5
e) 15

This one is extra tricky because it is asking you to use the crazy "@" equation twice, once for 10 @ 5, and again using that result as your "a" and the number 2 for your "b." Since we know we should start with what is in the parentheses, we will look first at 10 @ 5.

To find the value of 10 @ 5, all we need to do is replace "a" and "b" in the original equation with "10" and "5," like this:

$$a @ b = a / b + (a - b)$$
$$10 @ 5 = 10 / 5 + (10 - 5)$$
$$10 @ 5 = 2 + 5 = 7$$

Now we can replace 10 @ 5 with 7 to complete the second version of the given equation:

$$(10 @ 5) @ 2 = 7 @ 2$$
$$a @ b = a / b + (a - b)$$
$$7 @ 2 = 7 / 2 + (7 - 2) = 7 / 2 + 5 = 8 \tfrac{1}{2} \text{ or } 8.5$$

So the answer would be *b) 8.5.*

Symbol questions are manageable if you can get past your initial fears and take them step-by-step.

56 Trust in the Scale

Every once in a while, you might wonder how accurate an answer would be if you just look at a figure and guess what the angle measure is. Most of the time you can see whether an angle is greater than or less than 90 degrees, allowing you to eliminate an answer or two. And the one you are looking at might seem to be about half of 90 degrees, so you are tempted to peg its value at 45 degrees. Plus, you do not see that pesky "figures are not drawn to scale" message, and you are running out of time.

In short, go for it. The geometric figures on the SAT are drawn to scale unless the information in the question says otherwise. This does not mean you should eyeball every diagram to come up with the answer. It does mean this can be a useful strategy if you are in a pinch.

Knowing that diagrams are drawn to scale also can help you double-check your work if you are not sure you have completed a problem correctly. Rather than just fill in your answer choice, you can compare what you have for the value of a given angle or side and make sure it seems to be about the right value based on how the figure looks and the other values given. If not, you might need to go back to the drawing board.

57 Don't Assume the Prompt

The SAT can trick you without your realizing it. The easiest way it can do this is by leading you to believe that a prompt is asking for one thing when it's really asking for another.

Always read the prompts carefully, and circle what it's really asking you to do. You want to avoid filling in the blanks with what you think it's asking.

Guest Feature: Clark Steen

Always circle what the question is asking you to find. It is easy to do all the work correctly, then not answer the question that is being asked. For example, the SAT is famous for asking, "What is the value of $5x$?" because they know that you are asked in school to find the value of just x. If you circle what you are asked to find, you can make sure to answer the question they asked, not the question you assume they asked.

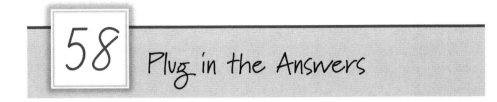

58 Plug in the Answers

It never hurts to plug the given answer options into the formula. If the question is relatively straight-forward, solving it through the process of elimination can be much quicker than trying to actually solve the problem from scratch.

> ## Guest Feature: Clark Steen
>
> If there are only real numbers in the answers, just take the answers and put them in for the value or variable or unknown they are asking for. For example, if they are asking how much money a person spent on one item in a list of three things, just stick in one of the answers, follow the directions in the problem, and see if the answer works. If not, try another answer.

59 Practice the Same Problems

Going over the same problem time and time again might prove to be annoying, but by practicing the same skill repeatedly, you are sure to perfect your skills. It is a much better use of your time to master a few skills than to barely dip your toes in a plethora of them.

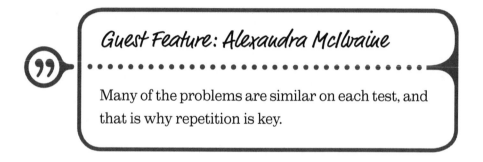

Guest Feature: Alexandra McIlvaine

Many of the problems are similar on each test, and that is why repetition is key.

CHAPTER 7

Writing Strategies: Crafting the Winning Essay

astering the essay section doesn't mean turning into the next *New York Times* best-selling author — it just requires you to learn how to frame an argument. This chapter will explain how the new essay is different as well as how to blow the judges away with your mad persuasion skills.

60 Practice the Same Problems

Toto, we aren't in Kansas anymore. The SAT is completely different, and the essay is no exception.

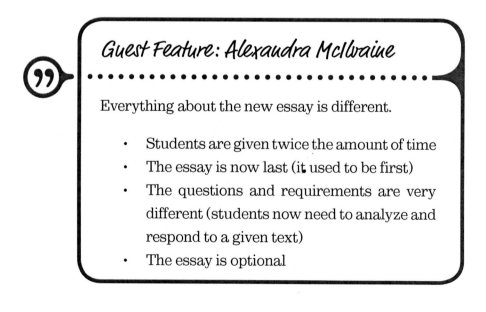

Guest Feature: Alexandra McIlvaine

Everything about the new essay is different.

- Students are given twice the amount of time
- The essay is now last (it used to be first)
- The questions and requirements are very different (students now need to analyze and respond to a given text)
- The essay is optional

It is important to verify with colleges in which a student is interested to determine whether or not the essay is necessary. We encourage all our students to prepare for the essay, unless they have succinct lists of colleges that all do not want the essay submitted. An advantage to the new SAT essay is that you can use the same format in your response to every essay topic. Once you have the outline, it becomes much easier to write the essay.

61 Let Your Book Be Judged By the Cover

The people who grade the SAT writing section do it quickly — as little as two minutes per essay — as is the case with all standardized tests. This means the grader doesn't pick apart your essay word by word but instead skims it and reads it with an eye out for certain criteria. If you're a natural writer, you should be able to hit these points without much trouble. However, writing is not always easy, and there are some things you can do to leave a great first impression.

First is the neatness factor. Studies have shown that the same essay will receive a higher score if it is easier to read. This is tough as many of us are now so used to computers that our handwriting is comparable to that of our infant siblings. However, it's worth your time to pay some attention to your handwriting.

Second, you should write a strong introduction. While graders will skim your essay, they are most likely to read the first paragraph closely, trying to gauge your overall writing ability by your sentence construction and the complexity of your ideas. Although you don't want to spend 30 minutes on that first paragraph, you want to spend a little extra time making it really shine.

One researcher at the Massachusetts Institute of Technology who did an analysis of sample essays found that longer essays received higher scores across the board. This may or may not be the case for essays overall, but it stands to reason that you can't earn a high score on an extremely short essay, because you wouldn't have enough words to explain your ideas adequately. So, don't be too brief.

Finally, don't make your paper too complex. You may feel a little pressure to write your "very best" by using big words and long, fancy sentences. While you do want to be using your A-list vocabulary and a wide variety of sentence structures, it's better to write in a clear, simple style.

As graders skim your essay, they will breeze through good, clear writing, figuring that the high score they want to give you based on your introduction still applies. Mistakes will stop them dead in their tracks, making them wonder if perhaps that score is a bit too high. Unclear sentences also will cause them to stop and try to figure out what you mean. And each time they stop, there is a good chance your score will drop. You want the graders to be able to skim effortlessly on their way to giving you the high score you deserve.

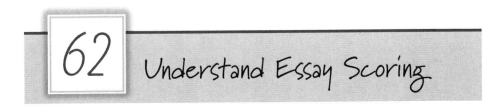

62 Understand Essay Scoring

Guest Feature: Clark Steen

This is perceived to be the least fair and least relevant section of the SAT. The Essay is optional, but many schools require it. The Essay is exactly what the students have learned to write in school: five paragraphs with a three-pronged thesis statement.

Students are judged on length, structure, and making sure that they use transitions and write neatly. The essay is a separate score, and most schools give it little weight. We recommend that students follow format, but then ignore the results. Anything above national average in scoring is just fine.

Your essay is reviewed twice, by separate graders, to ensure fairness. If it makes you feel any better, these graders are highly trained. While the judgments are made quickly, measures are in place to make sure someone else's bad day does not affect your score.

Here is what those graders look for as they assign scores from 1 to 4:

- **One:** You have demonstrated little to no comprehension of the material. You don't really explain the main idea, there are a lot of mistakes, and you don't provide any evidence.

- **Two:** You have demonstrated some comprehension of the material. You show that you understand a little bit of the main idea, but you're missing the main point. There are some errors and barely any use of textual evidence like quotes or paraphrases.

- **Three:** You understand the text just fine. There are hardly any errors, and you use appropriate evidence showing you comprehend the source text.

- **Four:** You are a rockstar. You completely understand the text, your argument is coherent and well supported, and you were a master of using evidence from the text to support your claim.

To see a thorough explanation of the scoring for each area of grading (reading, analysis, and writing), visit https://collegereadiness.collegeboard.org/sat/scores/understanding-scores/essay.

63 Don't Just Write — Plan and Edit, Too

Why is planning so important? First off, the average super-nervous test-taker tends to overlook it. She is so worried about getting enough words onto the paper within the time limit that she will just start scribbling and worry about what those words are later. Under these circumstances, the final product tends to lack the required focus on a particular point of view. Organization will be shoddy. Her ideas will start out slowly, then gain steam so that she is making her best points at the end, where the grader is least likely to notice them.

To avoid this fate, spend two to five minutes planning what you will say before you write. Then, make certain that you stick to your guns once you begin writing the essay. In 50 minutes, you do not have much time to start over if you have a better example or idea. Trust me; I wrote the beginning of two essays once and didn't finish either one. Only you can decide just how much you are able to commit to writing well in the time limit provided, so make a plan you know you can execute, and stick to it.

After planning, you must write. After that, another often-overlooked part of the process is editing. Yes, you are writing this longhand on a sheet of paper, not on a computer where you can make edits easily. However, you can still spend two or three minutes looking over your essay and using your eraser to fix grammatical errors. If needed, you can change a few words to make the essay read more smoothly, or you can clarify a particular point in the margins. At the very least, you can correct a few blatant errors.

Do not mark up your essay until it is illegible. A few reasonable edits, however, may help more than they will harm. Remember: you don't want grammatical errors or unclear sentences to trip up the person who grades your essay.

64 Practice Timed Essays

Although you may find it tedious, practice writing essays in 50 minutes. Learn how long it takes you to start writing; notice when you feel as though you are dragging and when you start to lose your concentration. Practice prompts are on **www.CollegeBoard.com**, or feel free to ask your English teacher for a prompt. This way, you will be prepared for anything that is thrown at you, and you will know you can write on various topics with ease.

Unlike some of the other sections on the SAT, where you can check the time in between questions, the essay section does not give you the kind of pauses that are convenient to figuring out how much time you have left. Instead, you can practice pausing in between paragraphs to gauge the time remaining in order to make certain you cover everything you want to cover. Writing the time the section ends on the top of the page can help you keep track of exactly how much time you have left. When you are told to put your pencil down, you don't want to panic because you're missing a whole paragraph.

65 Don't Write About Your Life

The SAT doesn't grade your essay based on what you know or what you've done. The graders want to see that you can present a coherent argument, string words together, and reason through complex ideas. The new SAT asks you to read a passage, explain how the author builds his or her argument, and then support that with evidence from the passage.

There is no need to include anything from your life — keep your essay about the passage and the passage only.

66 Expect the Prompt

You know that the prompt will be set up as follows:

- Read the provided excerpt/passage.
- Craft an explanation as to how the writer built an argument.
- Use evidence from the passage to support your explanation.

It's that simple, and this is what the prompt will be every time. You will never be asked to agree or disagree with a topic or position, so don't worry about practicing debating for the SAT.

67 Analyze Arguments

Next time you hear your parents arguing over who was supposed to clean the dishes, pay attention to how the arguments are framed. You know the SAT will require you to analyze an argument, so keep this perspective in the months leading up to the exam.

Who was more reasonable? Why? These are the same questions you will have to answer when you sit down in front of the prompt.

68 Choose the Best Examples

As a rule of thumb, you want three solid supporting ideas. You will explain each of these in one of the three body paragraphs, and you will use examples in each body paragraph. Start with what you think are the author's best arguments. That way, if you run out of time, you will not scrimp on explaining your best ideas.

69 Conquer the Blank Page

Now that we have settled on what ideas to put in the essay, the next hurdle is starting to write. Many students have trouble getting going on an essay, but having an idea of what you will write should help a lot. And since we have chosen our stance on the issue, we can start by writing a thesis statement, which as you have probably learned by now, will state the position we will argue throughout the essay.

A catchy first sentence can score you points and make your essay memorable. One safe bet is to restate the author's argument. From there, you might summarize the idea in your own words, then briefly introduce the three ideas you will explain in your body paragraphs.

While some people like to leave space for the introduction and come back to it later, I recommend writing the essay in order from beginning to end. You are working in pencil, so you can go back and change it if you need to. Writing the introduction first may help you organize your thoughts better as you progress through the essay.

70 Don't Write the Great American Novel

Guest Feature: Alexis Browsh

Quality over quantity is the name of the game here. Scorers judge the essay on three components only: reading, analysis, and writing. They want to see specific evidence of comprehension, a critical response to the prompt, and mature sentence construction and overall organization.

Use quotes and other evidence from the text to support your answer, and be sure to include some conclusions about the author's main idea and purpose. Also, throw in some sentence variety, college-level vocabulary, and clear essay organization, including transitions between paragraphs. Don't deliberate over every word choice and turn of phrase — you have a limited amount of time to write, and scorers are trained to quickly read dozens of essays per shift, scanning for specific benchmarks.

In other words, keep it short, smart, and sweet — like this tip.

71 Be Organized

A major factor in the way your essay is graded is the organization of the information. You may make a brilliant point, but if the grader can't find it because it's buried in paragraph 4, sentence 12, it doesn't do you any good.

You can organize your essay in several ways. The first is the basic way, with an introduction, three body paragraphs, and a conclusion. This simple essay is a surefire way to organize your thoughts in an understandable manner. Five paragraphs also will help ensure that you finish on time and make all your important points. You should devote the three body paragraphs to evidence supporting your stance on the prompt. When writing your introduction, briefly outline the ideas you will discuss in the three following paragraphs. (This is where your pre-planning comes in handy!) The fifth paragraph will state your conclusion.

This format is simple and effective and should serve most writers well. If you have major fears about the essay or just dislike writing in general, sticking with this proven format should guarantee you some success. An essay that adheres to this structure with very little explanation and a host of grammatical errors still is likely to earn an average score.

However, you don't *have* to do it that way. For instance, you could also write your essay chronologically. If you are comparing changes over time, this is a good way to construct your argument. Or you might have only a few ideas for the body paragraphs, but you want to explain each one more thoroughly. In that case, you might use the basic structure but with four, instead of five, paragraphs.

In any case, decide on a structure you feel comfortable with. The SAT does not have a rule for the way you should structure the essay so long as you hit the points the essay needs to contain. However, keep in mind that when you take risks, your chances of missing the mark increase. No matter what your organizational style, you always need to make sure you introduce the topic along with which side you are supporting; the rest of the essay can flow more freely.

Including transitions is also important; it can help your essay's coherency and unity, proving to the grader that you are capable of writing well. If you order your ideas chronologically, for example, you would use "first," "next," "then," and "last" to introduce each idea. If you present contrasting ideas, such as the points where you disagree with the quote, you would use words such as "however" and "nonetheless."

72 Use Sophisticated Arguments

This is more easily said than done, but essay graders do not just look for how many arguments and examples you make. They also look for how good these arguments are.

Guest Feature: Alexis Browsh

The essay scorers are sticklers for analysis. Showing you understood the prompt and the passage will earn at least an average score, but to get that 4/4, there needs to be evidence of deeper understanding. It is easy to fall into the trap of just summarizing the author's argument; use evidence from the author, but be sure to build from it to show an overall theme or purpose.

73 No Matter What, Finish

It is imperative that you finish your essay, even if you are running out of time. Most often, that means you will need to write a paragraph known as the conclusion, with at least three sentences summing up your ideas. Some essays can stand without a separate conclusion, and if you are used to writing an effective essay without one, don't let this suggestion stand in your way. However, if you find yourself with five minutes left and you feel as though you are not even close to done, you have to let go of what you are writing about and sum it up as best you can. Write in shorter sentences if you have to in order to make an impact without hurting your cause.

One way to make a more powerful ending is to bring up a universal truth in order to impress upon the grader the essay's main point. In your conclusion, bring in the world at large. Making a point about the human condition — or even just the way people interact with each other — is an almost surefire way to get the score you're looking for.

CHAPTER 8

The Writing Section: Mastering the Tips

Leave the texting lingo at home and channel your inner editor — the SAT Writing and Language Test will be asking you to be nit-picky about the ever-changing English language. You will be given passages with deliberate errors, and your job will be to improve them.

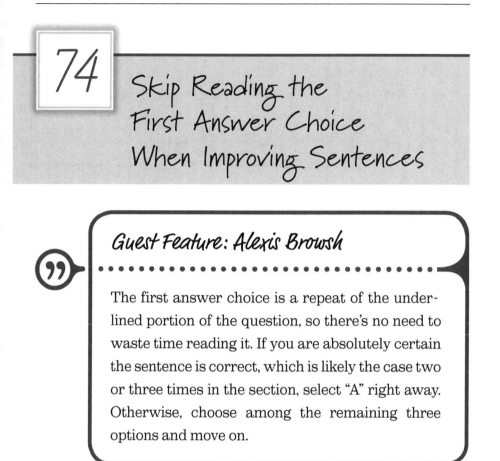

74 Skip Reading the First Answer Choice When Improving Sentences

Guest Feature: Alexis Browsh

The first answer choice is a repeat of the underlined portion of the question, so there's no need to waste time reading it. If you are absolutely certain the sentence is correct, which is likely the case two or three times in the section, select "A" right away. Otherwise, choose among the remaining three options and move on.

Knowing what is consistent from test to test can save you some time. One of those consistencies is the first answer choice in the "improving sentences" multiple-choice writing questions. In these questions, the first answer choice — answer choice *a)* —will always be the same as the original sentence.

In other words, if you feel the original sentence is perfectly fine in these questions, then answer choice *a)* will be a strong possibility. If you are sure the original sentence is not correct, then you can skip answer choice *a)* without even reading it. Some of these sentences will be long and convoluted, so you will save yourself some time by going straight to answer choice *b)*.

Try this method on a sample question:

While World War II was the cause of untold casualties on either side, it also spurred an economic boom *that lasted for decades after the* *violence ended.*

> *a) it also spurred an economic boom*
>
> *b) it also had spurred an economic boom*
>
> *c) it in addition caused to occur an economic boom*
>
> *d) they also spurred an economic boom*
>
> *e) it also spurred an economical boom*

My first thought upon reading this sentence is that it sounded pretty good, so I kept answer choice *a)* in my mind as a possibility. I was not completely sure it could not be improved, though, so I continued reading through the answer choices. I did not bother reading over *a)*, however, because I knew already that it was the same as the original sentence.

Answer choice *b)* changed "spurred" to "had spurred," which is not correct in this sentence. Answer choice *c)* changed and added phrases to the sentence, making it wordier without improving it grammatically. Answer choice *d)* changed "it" to "they," an incorrect move because "World War II," the subject, is singular. Finally, *e)* changed "economic" to "economical," which is not necessary. Since none of the other changes improved the sentence, I stuck with my first choice, *a)*.

75 Know What Could Be Wrong

In most of the questions in this section, the errors you are looking for will be grammatical in nature: choosing "its" or "it's" and using the proper conjunction, for example. The improving-sentences and identifying-sentence-error questions will include only grammatical concepts. The errors will not be in areas such as using the wrong word or making an assertion that is false or illogical. So even if something looks odd to you in this section, if it isn't a grammatical error, don't worry about it.

When it comes to the paragraphs, however, you could be asked to make improvements in ways that go beyond grammar. In fact, on these questions, the paragraph may be grammatically correct. You may be asked to choose a sentence that would improve the paragraph by making a point more clear. Or, you may be asked to smooth the transition between ideas in a sentence by choosing a phrase to add. Additionally, you may be asked to pick the best revision of a given sentence that is grammatically correct but illogical or awkward in some way.

To recap, sentences are all grammar, while the paragraph questions will involve grammar and beyond. Don't go looking for non-grammatical errors in the sentences, and don't get too stuck on grammar in the paragraphs. This takes practice, so be sure to go through a series of practice tests so that you are familiar with the kinds of errors that show up in each question type.

Here's an example of an "improving paragraphs" question that goes beyond grammar:

(1) Corn was known as "maize" by the Native Americans who first cultivated it. (2) It was a mainstay of their diet long before newcomers to the American continent learned to grow it. (3) At first, maize consisted of tiny cobs growing on wild plants. (4) The cobs got bigger. (5) Now a cob of corn is quite large.

Which of the following additions to sentence 4 (reproduced below) would fit best in the paragraph?

The cobs got bigger.

a) Corn started to grow bigger and taste better, so that more people wanted to eat it.

b) Early farmers planted seeds from the largest cobs, and the cobs grew bigger with successive plantings.

c) Each year, the cobs got bigger.

    d) The cobs grew bigger, and Native Americans learned to cook it in different ways.

    e) Farmers made the cobs bigger.

The best answer here is going to make a smooth transition between the two sentences surrounding the sentence in question. The sentence before is talking about how the cobs were originally small, while the one after is about how large the cobs are now. Therefore, the correct answer is *b)*. This sentence explains how the cobs went from small to big over the years.

Of the other answer choices, the most appealing is probably *d)*. This answer choice does seem to add to the paragraph and fits the topic at hand. However, it returns to the ideas brought up early in the paragraph, which don't fit in these later sentences. These answer choices are all grammatically correct, but some contribute more to the paragraph's meaning and structure than others do. That will often be the case when you are asked to improve paragraphs.

76 Interpret Grammar Widely

Grammatical issues on the SAT encompass some writing problems that you might not see as grammatically incorrect. Your English teachers probably have discouraged these things, but you might not have considered them to be "wrong." We will look at a few of them:

- **Wordiness:** Using more words than are needed to make a particular point. Could the underlined part of the following sentence be removed, for instance? "Her favorite song was one that was sung by the late Nat King Cole." Yes, you can take out these words without changing the meaning of the sentence. So even if you thought the original sentence sounded grammatically correct, an answer choice that removes those words would be better because it lacks unnecessary words.

- **Passive voice:** You would not say, "The sandwich was just eaten by me." So why would you say, "*The Odyssey* was written by Homer"? Your English teacher probably has urged you to avoid passive sentences such as these. On the SAT, passive voice should be considered incorrect. The correct forms would be "I ate the sandwich" and "Homer wrote *The Odyssey*."

- **Idiomatic expressions:** Some phrases in the English language go a certain way just because that is the way they are. If you were learning English as a foreign language, for instance, you would simply have to memorize them, because there is no consistent rule. If a sentence uses one of these expressions incorrectly, it's an error — even if you can't pinpoint why. Here's an example of a popular idiom: "Look outside — it's raining cats and dogs!"

77 Make Sure Everything Matches

Guest Feature: Alexis Browsh

If there's one grammatical concept to master for the SAT, it's agreement. Subject-verb, pronoun-antecedent, verb tense ... always check that the words throughout the sentence match. If there are three verbs in a row, make sure they all have the same ending or parallel structure. Plural subjects take plural verbs, singular subjects take singular verbs, and the same goes for pronouns and the words they replace. Be especially careful of extra words thrown in between, for example, the subject and verb — these can draw your attention away from the true case of the subject or pronoun.

Avoiding grammatical errors — or in this case finding them — is often a matter of making sure all parts of a sentence or paragraph match in a variety of ways. If you think an SAT grammar question sounds perfect the way it is, double-check by making sure each of these areas is in agreement throughout the sentence or paragraph:

- **Subject – verb:** "The girls wants to go to the park." The subject and verb of a sentence both must be either plural or singular, so you would replace "wants" with "want" (or "girls" with "girl") to make the subject and verb agree. These can be more difficult when a phrase separates the subject from the verb, so you sometimes need to isolate the two parts and make sure they match. Try this one, for instance: "The girls, who were in agreement with their teacher, wants to go to the park." "Wants" may agree with "teacher," but that is not the subject. "Wants" needs to agree with "girls," the subject.

- **Pronoun – noun:** "The student wanted to go on the field trip, so they brought back their permission forms." "Student" is singular, but "they" is plural. In this case, you could replace "they" with "he," "she," or "he or she."

- **Noun – noun:** "Jeanne and Cathy are both an engineer." Since we are talking about two of them, the end of the sentence should read "are both engineers."

- **Verb tense:** "He wanted so badly to go to medical school that he takes out a loan from his ex-wife's parents." This sentence starts in past tense with "wanted," then shifts to present tense with "takes." Verb tense should be consistent throughout. Replace "takes" with "took."

- **Pronoun shift:** "If you study hard, one can't help but succeed on the SAT." This sentence moves from second person, "you," to third person, "one." Either would be correct, but you must use it in both places in the sentence.

- **Parallelism (items in a list):** "She decided to leave because her classes were boring, her bank account was empty, and she didn't have a boyfriend anyway." One of the items in this list does not look like the others. To make them all look the same, you might rephrase the last item from "she didn't have a boyfriend anyway" to "her love life was dull." That way, all the items look the same.

Looking for all of these kinds of agreement will be particularly helpful on "identifying error" questions such as this one:

Running for exercise have many health benefits, but it can also cause
A   B   C   D
knee pain and injury. No error.
*   E*

The directions will ask you to choose the letter that corresponds to an underlined error. In this case, you may have thought that a few things sounded wrong as you read the sentence. However, the most glaring error turns up at answer choice *b)* "have." That is a plural form of the verb, while the subject "running for exercise" is singular. In the "identifying error" questions, you do not have to worry about fixing the problem; you just have to pinpoint what is wrong.

78 Look For Common Problems

Some issues show up time after time in the grammar questions, and they aren't always the ones you would think of as major grammatical problems. The more subtle the problem, the harder it is to find, right? Look for these common SAT problems as you take the test. You're bound to find a few errors you wouldn't have otherwise.

- **What is after the comma:** "Eating voraciously, the veal chops were delicious to Jeremy." In a sentence with an introductory phrase, the person or thing the phrase refers to should come directly after the comma. In this case, it was Jeremy who was eating, not the veal. So it should read: "Eating voraciously, Jeremy found the veal chops delicious."

- **Bad comparisons:** "Elaine's car was faster than her brother." Well, her car probably does go faster than her brother can run, but more likely this sentence means to compare her car to her "brother's car," which should replace "brother."

- **The wrong connecting word:** "Maribel likes jazz and Jaime prefers rock." The connecting word "and" connects two similar ideas. In this case, the two people like two different things, so a connecting word that expresses contrast would be more appropriate. Replace "and" with "but."

- **Comma splice:** "The dog show was fascinating, each breed had its own story." This is two sentences treated as if they were one. To fix, you could replace the comma with a semicolon (;). Or you could add a connecting word after the comma, such as "because." Finally, you can replace the comma with a period and create two sentences.

79 | Be Careful with "No Change" Answers

It may seem reasonable to choose the "no change" or "no error" answer option. However, SAT prep expert Justin Berkman decided to analyze just how often this answer choice was the correct answer. He studied four SATs released by the College Board and found that this answer choice is the least likely to be correct[1].

Of course, every test is different, and the correct answer choices will vary, but he warns test-takers to be wary of this answer choice. If you have a ton of "no change" answers in a row, you might be off track.

This tidbit of information can also aid you in shot-in-the-dark guesses. If you have no clue, you're better off guessing one of the other answer choices as it's statistically more likely to be correct.

That being said, don't be scared of the "no change" answer choice – it'll be correct sometimes — just not every time.

80 | Memorize Grammar Rules

Instead of listening to Swift's new album during study hall, pester your English teacher for grammar lessons instead. Your brain is hard-wired

---

1 Berkman, 2015.

to understand categories much better than single things. So, if you learn an over-arching grammar rule, you're much better off than learning one specific instance of it.

Here's an example:

Grammar Rule: Use a comma to connect two ideas.

   Example: I don't like spaghetti, and I hate drinking milk.

Now, you could just memorize that a comma goes before "and" (though this would still lead you astray every once in a while), but that disregards all of the other connecting words such as "nor," "but," and "which" to name a few.

If you commit the general grammar rules to memory, you will do much better if a scenario you've never specifically encountered before arises.

Guest Feature: Alexandra McIlvaine

One of the greatest challenges in the Writing Section is grammar. When was the last time someone asked you to define when to use a semicolon? The nitty-gritty grammar rules are important and often require the most time to master. This section is very repetitive, though, and when students take the time to break down the different types of questions into categories, it becomes much easier and faster to answer the questions.

81 Study the Chicago Manual of Style

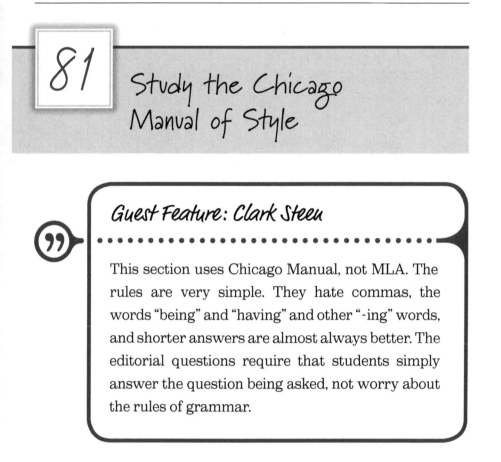

Guest Feature: Clark Steen

This section uses Chicago Manual, not MLA. The rules are very simple. They hate commas, the words "being" and "having" and other "-ing" words, and shorter answers are almost always better. The editorial questions require that students simply answer the question being asked, not worry about the rules of grammar.

To read up on the Chicago Manual of Style, visit **www.chicago manualofstyle.org/home.html**. You can also follow them on Twitter (@ChicagoManual) for helpful tips.

CHAPTER 9

Critical Reading: Word-Play Strategies

From textbooks to Facebook posts, you are no newbie to reading. You've been doing it for many years, so all you have to do now is focus in on some key skills that the SAT is testing for:

1. **Command of evidence:** You'll be asked to find evidence in a passage, identify how the author uses that evidence to support the claim being made, and occasionally find a connection between a graphic and the passage it's paired with.

2. **Words in context:** You'll be asked to use context clues to find out the meaning of a word or phrase as well as deciding how a word choice shapes and/or enhances the passage.

3. **Analysis in History/Social Studies and Science:** You'll be asked to examine hypotheses, interpret data, and consider the implications of that data.

This chapter is going to help you figure out how to master these skills, and we'll also help you learn exactly what to expect, which as you know by now, is half the battle.

82 Know What Kinds of Passages to Expect

As you know, the Reading section of the SAT is 65 minutes, and it has 52 questions. That's useful to know, but a bit more in-depth knowledge will serve you well.

Thankfully, we do know what kinds of passages will be on this section of the test. All of the passages are real, published works. You can expect single passages that might have accompanying graphics (like charts).

There will be one literary fiction passage that will be taken from either a short story or a novel. Examples of literary fiction include:

- The Great Gatsby (1925) by F. Scott Fitzgerald
- The Goldfinch (2013) by Donna Tartt
- To Kill a Mockingbird (1960) by Harper Lee
- The Handmaid's Tale (1986) by Margaret Atwood
- The Kite Runner (2003) by Khaled Hosseini
- The Catcher in the Rye (1951) by J.D. Salinger

It might be a good idea to pick up a few literary fiction novels from the library to get comfortable with the kind of texts you will see on the exam. I'm sure your English teacher will have a few suggestions for you.

The rest of the passages will be nonfiction informational passages covering the subjects of history, social studies, and science. There will be one passage taken from the founding documents of the United States.

The purpose of the passages will be one of the following:

1. It might be trying to tell a story
2. It could be making an argument
3. It might explain a study or an experiment

83 Know What Kinds of Questions to Expect

Now that you know what kinds of passages will be on the test, it might help to know what kinds of questions will be asked about those passages. According to the helpful video on the College Board's website[1], the questions in this section will ask you to do the following:

1. Understand what the passage is saying — directly or indirectly
2. Think about how the author of the passage expresses what he or she means
3. Draw conclusions and make connections between several passages or between passages and graphics

Now that you know what to expect, how the heck can you study for it? By reading every book in your school library? We have good news — and it doesn't involve speed-reading and no sleep! Check out the next tip.

84 Prepare a Study Strategy

So, you know what they're testing for, but how on earth do you study for this? Well, surprise surprise — going over sample questions and taking practice tests will greatly improve your final performance in this section.

---

1 **https://collegereadiness.collegeboard.org/sat/inside-the-test/reading**.

Check out the sample questions on the College Board's website: **https:// collegereadiness.collegeboard.org/sample-questions/reading**.

Beyond practicing though, there are some strategies you can use to study more efficiently. SAT expert Allen Cheng explains that the reading section is designed to trip you up — you're asked to choose the "most likely" answer, and this usually ends up with you narrowing the options down to two answers, and then you guess the wrong one. The SAT creators know this, but if you can learn what types of questions to expect, you can learn strategies to solve them.

Cheng goes on to suggest that you learn how to cut out three wrong answers. He explains:

> ...the SAT always has one unambiguous answer. This has a huge implication for the strategy you should use to find the right SAT Reading answer.

> Here's the other way to see it: **Out of the 4 answer choices, 3 of them have something that is totally wrong about them.** Only 1 answer is 100% correct, which means the other 3 are 100% wrong.[2]

So, instead of getting tripped up by trying to narrow down the answer choices, look at it like this — only one answer is completely correct. This strategy can completely change the way you go about studying for this part of the SAT.

---

2 Cheng, 2015.

85 Choose Your Reading Method

You need to find your best order of operations for when you sit down to take this test. A huge part of that is deciding if you want to read the passage first or the questions first. Let's look to expert Clark Steen for some advice.

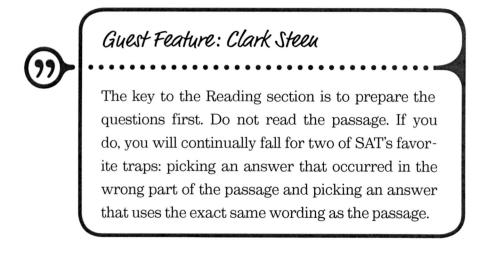

Guest Feature: Clark Steen

The key to the Reading section is to prepare the questions first. Do not read the passage. If you do, you will continually fall for two of SAT's favorite traps: picking an answer that occurred in the wrong part of the passage and picking an answer that uses the exact same wording as the passage.

86 Read in Chunks

While some students will find the previous method useful, others might prefer what SAT expert Alexandra McIlvaine explains as "chunking."

Guest Feature: Alexandra McIlvaine

Many students without professional instruction will read the entire passage and proceed to answer the questions. Sounds logical, right? For many students who read more slowly, have trouble retaining information, or have trouble focusing, this strategy can be ineffective.

One strategy we implement is called "chunking." In chunking, the student is asked to read the first two paragraphs, then jump over to the questions to answer as many as possible that pertain to the information they just read, then the process is repeated until the passage is finished and the questions are all answered. Breaking the passage into chunks can help a student maintain focus, answer more questions in a shorter amount of time when time is of the essence, and it does not require students to remember nearly as much detail as they move through the passage. Chunking is one of many techniques that we offer to our students and is simply a taste of our "secret sauce."

87 Don't Read the Entire Passage

Being thorough is really great when it comes to things like doing your taxes and baking a cheesecake, but when it comes to reading the passages in the Reading section of the SAT — well, it might not be your best choice. Master the art of skimming to maximize your time and to avoid getting caught up in extraneous information.

Guest Feature: Clark Steen

Once the questions are prepped, students need only read the first and last sentence of each paragraph to find all of the information for the questions. Getting caught in the middle of a paragraph leads to disaster. The only time to read the middle of a paragraph is if there is a line reference specifically sending the student to that spot.

All answers must be within two lines of whatever reference point they are given. When you find an answer, go to that question immediately. Do not keep reading. That leads to finding answers in the wrong part of the passage. The temptation, taught to many students in school, is that they must read more when they do not understand. Because of the method outlined, reading more obviously sets

> you up to be misled. Critical Reading is not really about understanding what is being read; it is about matching what has been said with an answer that says the same thing, but in synonyms.

All answers must be within two lines of whatever reference point they are given. When you find an answer, go to that question immediately. Do not keep reading. That leads to finding answers in the wrong part of the passage. The temptation, taught to many students in school, is that they must read more when they do not understand. Because of the method outlined, reading more obviously sets you up to be misled. Critical Reading is not really about understanding what is being read; it is about matching what has been said with an answer that says the same thing, but in synonyms.

88 Build Your Vocabulary

Expanding your vocabulary is a slow process, but there are strategies you can use to get the most bang for your buck. The course "Building a Better Vocabulary," put out by The Great Courses®, provides some strategies for maximizing your lexicon quickly and efficiently.

Professor and language expert Kevin Flannigan explains that it's not really worthwhile to memorize individual words. Instead, practice learning word roots and morphology. Morphology is the fancy word for the history and structure of words.

Here's an example:

The Latin root "spect" means "to look or to see." Why would it be useful to know this? Well, because the following words have that root in it, and you can easily gather the gist of what they mean based off that knowledge:

- Spectacles
- Inspector
- Spectator
- Speculate
- Retrospect

Here's another example. The Latin root "auto" means "self" or "same", so the following words have something to do with the self or with sameness:

- Autograph
- Autobiography
- Automobile

- Automotive
- Autodidact
- Automatic
- Autocratic
- Autonomy
- Automate
- Autopilot

Professor Flannigan goes on to explain that by learning one root, you open yourself up to learn about 10 new words. That's 10x more words than you'd learn if you tried to memorize them one-by-one. The other great thing about using this strategy — if you come across a word you don't know on the SAT, you can try to pick it apart and see if you can draw up some meaning from the roots. That will lead you at least to an educated guess, which is far better than going in blind.

A great tool to start practicing with morphology and word roots is the website Membean (**www.membean.com**). Check out their root trees here: **www.membean.com/educator/wordroots**.

89 Read Whenever You Can

No matter which skill you're trying to improve, you should read books that you consider to be above your reading level, and you may have to read books that don't particularly interest you.

To practice for the reading-comprehension questions, try to read a wide variety of fairly complex writing, both fiction and nonfiction. Try to read quickly and summarize the works to yourself as you read. Pick up a pencil and highlight the key points. If you do this regularly, you will improve your reading comprehension in two ways. First, you are learning to read quickly while also keeping track of major points. Second, you are familiarizing yourself with the advanced type of writing you might see on the test.

Reading in general helps you grasp words and the way they're used. When you come to a more complex sentence on the test, you may be able to deconstruct the meaning if you are aware of the way authors utilize the language via context clues. Many classics in literature are written in a different style of language than we speak today. Being able to read such works is critical.

90 Find the Main Point or Idea

A common critical-reading question will ask you to find the main idea of the passage. In this type of question, you determine the answer that best represents *all* the information in the passage. If you have asked yourself the right questions, you should have an idea of what you are looking for.

The easiest way to tackle this type of question is to have a sentence already in your head about what you think the main idea is so that you can find the answer quickly. Then, look for a comparable answer choice. Small details should not be part of the correct "main idea" answer, so even if an answer is technically correct, be sure to eliminate it if it doesn't summarize the text as a whole.

91 Know How to Choose the Best Title

Another type of reading-comprehension question will ask you to pick the best title for the selected reading. Choosing a title is very similar to identifying the main idea, because a title should also touch on the main idea of the passage.

Much like main-idea questions, you will find that some answer choices are too specific to be considered good titles, focusing on details instead of the overall idea. Other answer choices will encompass ideas that are too broad to be a good fit for the passage.

Understand that these kinds of questions are always a stretch. At times, it may seem like the "best answer" is equally as bad as the other options. These are questions in which you have to think like the person who wrote the test and work only with the words on the page. Thinking like a student who reads more into everything than what is there can keep you from succeeding. Practicing questions is a better way to understand what the test is looking for rather than attacking the question blindly.

92 Annotate, But Don't Overdo It

Reading with a pencil is a good way to make those minutes count during the exam. We have talked about reading for the gist and having an idea in your head of what the passage is about. For other questions, however, it helps to have a handle on some details. That's where your pencil comes in.

Annotation is when you mark things in the passage as you read. Although it may seem unnecessary, annotating a passage is an excellent way to save time when you go back to the passage to answer questions. If you have marked things that stand out as important or "big picture," you can find them quickly without trying to memorize them as you read.

Annotation is particularly helpful with longer passages, especially if your tactic is to read the passage before the questions. It also can be helpful on narrative passages. Noting clues to the meaning of the work can help you later. Take this passage, for instance:

The sun should set shortly over the bay. Jesse knew this, but she didn't head for home just yet. Her father wouldn't understand why she loved the night air so much. He didn't ever take walks with her and her mother at night to watch the stars dance over the ocean. He would only stay inside with his precious books. That's what professors do, her mother had told her when she was young, and for years she thought that was what her father made a living doing: staying inside with his books.

The cool wind blew across the bay, soft ripples from the wakes further out sent salt into her face. There were coos in the distance from the reed birds, licks along the bottoms of the boats at their moors, and a plop every now and then as a fish re-entered the water. All Jesse heard was the absence of her mother.

She and her mother used to revere the noises as their private symphony. The egret that lived around the corner their pet, they would revel in the natural way the bird conducted with his bobbing neck, gracing the pair with his presence. His dexterous steps breaking the glass beneath him kept her and her mother enthralled for hours. That was before the egret flew away. He must have only loved her mother, or been there to make her smile, for they had both forsaken her.

It had been almost a year now that they had lived at the beach house. Her father had sold the house with the yard and the memories to live in the beach shack where he had no memories. Jesse was left alone with hers now in her silence. The clouds danced across the moon with no reservations and illustrated the eerie feeling that Jesse had experienced since last summer. Her mother's illness had ravished her once-beautiful features before stealing her away. Only Jesse and her tears gazed out at the once-beautiful twilight now. There was no laughter, except for the seagull saying its goodnights — which Jesse couldn't hear.

If I am reading for the gist, as I should be, I might say that this passage is about a girl (or perhaps a woman) remembering her mother while sitting near a bay at dusk. I also would note that she seems to have a strained relationship with her father. This passage appears to be fiction and is full of imagery. Its purpose is not to inform, but to entertain or perhaps to reveal some truth about human nature.

Now, we will look at some details we might have felt were important enough to underline so that we could find them later.

The sun should set shortly over the bay. Jesse knew this, but she didn't head for home just yet. <u>Her father wouldn't understand why she loved the night air so much.</u> He didn't ever take walks with her and her mother at night to watch the stars dance over the ocean. He would only <u>stay inside with his precious books. That's what professors do,</u> her mother had told her when she was young, and for years she thought that was what her father made a living doing: staying inside with his books.

The cool wind blew across the bay, soft ripples from the wakes further out sent salt into her face. There were coos in the

Imagery

distance from the reed birds, licks along the bottoms of the boats at their moors, and a plop every now and then as a fish re-entered the water. All Jesse heard was the absence of her mother.

She and her mother used to revere the noises as their private symphony. The egret that lived around the corner their pet, they would revel in the natural way the bird conducted with his bobbing neck, gracing the pair with his presence. His dexterous steps breaking the glass beneath him kept her and her mother enthralled for hours. That was before the egret flew away. He must have only loved her mother, or been there to make her smile, for they had both forsaken her.

Mother gone? Egret a symbol?

It had been almost a year now that they had lived at the beach house. Her father had sold the house with the yard and the memories to live in the beach shack where he had no memories. Jesse was left alone with hers now in her silence. The clouds danced across the moon with no reservations and illustrated the eerie feeling that Jesse had experienced since last summer. Her mother's illness had ravished her once-beautiful features before stealing her away. Only Jesse and her tears gazed out at the once-beautiful twilight now. There was no laughter, except for the seagull saying its goodnights — which Jesse couldn't hear.

As I read the story, I noted parts that seemed to explain what was going on. I didn't dwell on the imagery or decorative language, although I did note that the egret may be a symbol of something. I also noted one paragraph that was almost purely imagery. I wondered throughout if Jesse's mother had died, and when I saw a sentence that showed she had, I double-underlined it because it seemed very important.

These markings don't seem like much, but they can be a useful guide when I get to the questions, helping me find information amid this narrative's flowery language. Looking at a few main highlighted points is way less intimidating than looking at a huge chunk of text.

93 Pay Attention to "Not" Questions

A question that includes the word *not* often throws test-takers off. What you are looking for on these, however, is the answer choice that is *not* present in the passage. The test-makers know human nature will lead students astray on these questions, which is why you see them written this way. Let's try one based on the previous passage:

What is NOT one of the changes mentioned in the passage?

- *Jesse's mom has died.*
- *Jesse's father sold their house.*
- *Jesse spends a lot of time completely alone.*
- *The egret has left the bay.*
- *Jesse and her father are getting to know each other better.*

This question exemplifies the problem of reading the questions too quickly, because it asks for a change that was *not* mentioned in the passage. Clearly, many things were not mentioned in the passage, so the best way to approach this is by choosing between the answer choices, starting with *a)*.

If I look back at my notes, I double-underlined what seemed like a crucial sentence. In that sentence, the author says that "her mother's illness" had hurt her "before stealing her away." Although it is not directly stated, it is clear that Jesse's mother died. If I were to approach this question hastily, I might be so excited to see this fact that I had thought was important right there in answer choice *a)* that I would choose it. But this is a "not" question, so *a)* is *not* the answer.

You can move on to answer choice b) now that you have eliminated a). This one is a little easier because it is more explicit in the text. "Her father had sold the house" is worded almost exactly the same as answer choice b) and conveys the same idea. I also had underlined this key point. Since it is in the text, we can eliminate it as a correct answer.

Answer choice *c)* is not directly stated but is apparent by the language the author uses to describe Jesse and how she spends her time. Words such as "absence," "alone," and "silence" in the passage allude to her solitude. I want to eliminate this one based on these references, but I am not totally sure. I will keep it in contention, then, as I check the other answer choices.

As we progress to answer choice *d)*, we see that a sentence in the passage says, "That was before the egret flew away." Using my notes, I know where to look for this detail because I have noted in which paragraph I would find the egret. I can eliminate *d)*.

This leaves *e)*. The idea that Jesse and her father are getting to know each other better is certainly not in the passage because the author highlights the fact that Jesse's dad does not understand her. It makes no reference to them spending time together; if it had, I certainly would have underlined it. Answer choice *e)* is a far better choice than *c)*, which I was still considering, so I will choose *e)*, the right answer.

With my notes as a guide and my careful reading of the question, this "not" question was difficult, but manageable.

94 Know the Writing Tricks

Particularly for fiction passages, SAT questions may ask you what kind of literary tools the author has employed in his or her writing. Here is a potential question that would encompass a variety of literary devices:

The author employs all of these literary devices EXCEPT:

1. *Personification*
2. *Simile*
3. *Imagery*
4. *Alliteration*
5. *Onomatopoeia*

For those who are not familiar with or don't remember these terms, here's a little review:

- **Personification:** Giving an object (or sometimes animals) human-like values or qualities.

- **Simile:** A comparison of two things using "like" or "as." (A metaphor is also a comparison but is made without the use of "like" or "as.")

- **Imagery:** A descriptive picture of a scene using language; can entail any of the five senses: sight, smell, sound, taste, or touch.

- **Alliteration:** A series of similar sounds or identical letters in one phrase.

- **Onomatopoeia:** A word that imitates a sound.

FIVE SENSES LINE ICONS

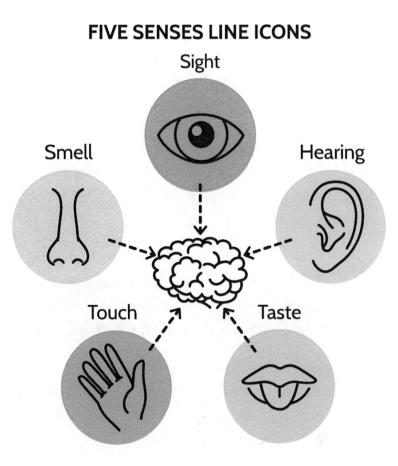

We will decide on the correct answer based on what the literary devices mean. Note that the question is looking for the device the author did *not* use.

Answer choice *a) Personification* is found in multiple places in the text. The first occurrence is at the end of the second paragraph: "All Jesse heard was the absence of her mother." This sentence suggests that "absence," a feeling, is capable of emitting a sound. A second example of personification occurs in the last paragraph. "The clouds danced" is a personification because dancing is something humans do, or perhaps animals, but not inanimate objects such as clouds.

Moving on to answer choice *b) Simile*, you would need to skim the passage for a comparison using "like" or "as." You will not find any. An example of a simile that would have fit in the reading is "Jesse was like the ugly duckling, all alone." Still, to be sure you did not miss something, continue to skim the rest of the answers.

The next possible choice is *c) Imagery*. The third paragraph about the egret is language that paints a picture, which I had marked in my notes. Creating a descriptive portrait of the landscape or what is going on in the scene constitutes imagery.

The choice of *d) Alliteration* is also easy to spot. The first sentence, "The sun should set shortly over the bay," has alliteration in it. The repeated "s" at the beginning of the words fits the definition of alliteration. If the same sound appears in a passage, this is alliteration as well.

Finally, *e) Onomatopoeia* is also found. In this passage, the "coos ... from the reed birds" count as onomatopoeia. A "coo" is a word that is the same as the sound it represents. By reviewing each answer choice, you have made certain that *b)* is the right answer.

Questions that involve "not" or "except" can take time because you must go through each answer choice. With patience, however, you can answer them correctly.

Chapter 10

SAT Mindset: How to Be Calm and Collected

You have a lot of preparing and practicing to do, but don't forget to be calm and collected. This chapter is full of super easy tips to make sure you have the best shot at getting your best score, and they don't require much practice. We promise.

95 Register for Two Test Dates

Instead of signing up for one test date, go ahead and do two. It takes off the pressure and calms your anxieties.

Guest Feature: Alexandra McIlvaine

We encourage families to register for two test dates up front so that the students know that their entire educational futures are not resting on the scores resulting from the first SAT date. For students that experience testing anxiety beyond the general nerves, we partner them with an instructor who has a background in Psychology and/or Behavior Analysis. We provide relaxation strategies to perform silently throughout the test, and for those with extreme anxiety, we advocate for those students to request special testing accommodations.

96 Prepare the Night Before

Don't wake up a frantic mess the day of the test — have everything ready to go. This way, even if the worst thing *ever* happens (you hit snooze 10 times too many), you can literally grab your bag and go.

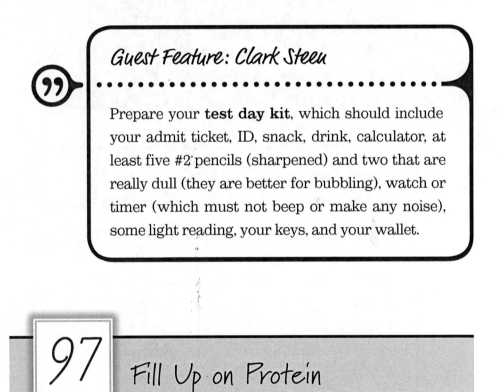

Guest Feature: Clark Steen

Prepare your **test day kit**, which should include your admit ticket, ID, snack, drink, calculator, at least five #2 pencils (sharpened) and two that are really dull (they are better for bubbling), watch or timer (which must not beep or make any noise), some light reading, your keys, and your wallet.

97 Fill Up on Protein

Donuts are good, we know, but filling up on substantial food can sharpen your mind on this extra important day.

Guest Feature: Clark Steen

Food matters. Eat a breakfast loaded with protein and short on carbohydrates. Carbs trigger a diabetic reaction that makes you sleepy. We recommend eggs or other meats. Avoid pancakes, cereal, oatmeal, waffles, etc. If you must have some toast or other carbs, slow down absorption with some butter.

98 Avoid Screen Time

Studies have shown that exposing yourself to electronic gadgets before bedtime can totally ruin your sleep cycle. According to Sleep.org, the blue light suppresses melatonin, the hormone responsible for controlling your circadian rhythm.[1]

Instead of watching the latest YouTube video, try opening up an actual book. Give your brain some time to unwind — at least the night before your big day.

---

1 National Sleep Foundation, no date provided.

99 Attend Practice Sessions

OK, OK, we get it. Lay off the advice to practice. But really — the foundation to success in SAT preparation is simulating the test experience and evaluating how you did. The only way to get better is to practice and figure out what you need to improve on.

Guest Feature: Alexandra McIlvaine

Educational Services offers Proctored Practice Tests on Saturday and Sunday mornings in our office to help students acclimate to the test center environment, which is full of distractions like coughing and tapping of pencils. Our Proctored Practice Tests also allow students to experience exact timing and the full-length fatigue factor. Typically, after a student has taken the full-length exam on multiple occasions under test-center-like conditions, it becomes easier to maintain calm during the real test because the students will have developed a routine.

We have three Philadelphia-area offices located in St. David's, PA (near Villanova University), Wyndmoor, PA (near Chestnut Hill) and Chadds Ford, PA (near Longwood Gardens). We currently have students from central Pennsylvania, New Jersey,

New York, Delaware and have previously worked with students all over the country. For families who are not within driving distance, we offer instruction through Skype. Skype still allows for face-to-face interaction to develop the rapport between student and instructor, and the instructor can still visually explain how to work through a question step by step.

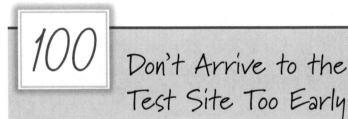

100 Don't Arrive to the Test Site Too Early

There is such a thing as being too early when it comes to the big day. Arriving early and sitting for too long can bring up feelings of anxiety and jitteriness — not to mention the distractions from other test takers.

Guest Feature: Clark Steen

Do not get to the test too early. People mill around and complain. Go into the test site 15 minutes before you are supposed to arrive, check in, and do some light reading. Any reading will get the juices flowing to the brain and get you set for the test. You may, if you wish, bring a few SAT/ACT warm-up problems to sharpen your brain.

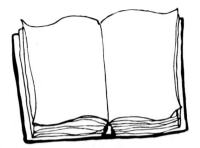

Conclusion

There you have it — 100 ways to help you get your best score on the SAT! Our last and final tip to hit that lovely number of 101 is:

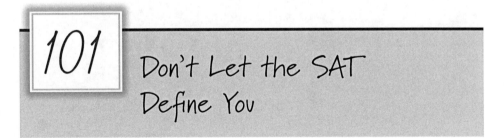

101 Don't Let the SAT Define You

At the end of the day, don't let a test score determine your value. You are smart, you are capable, and if you read this book all the way to the end, you are obviously motivated. Some people just aren't good test takers, and that's OK.

You have plenty of time to find where your passion lies, and the last thing you should do is let the SAT control your life. Do your best, and let the rest fall into place.

Happy studying!

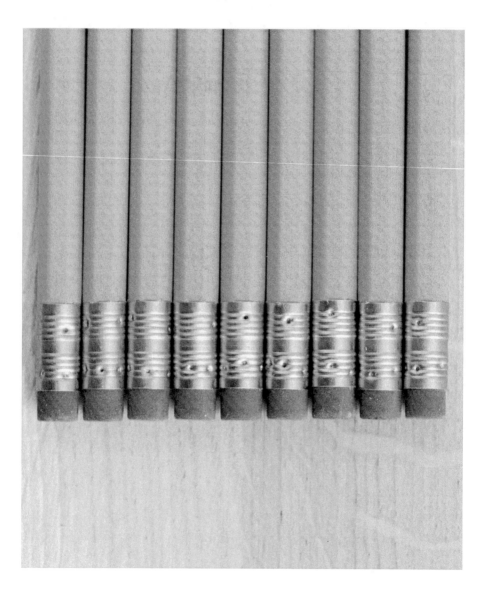

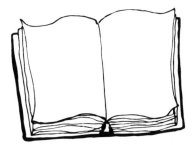

Glossary

Annotate: To add notes to text or a diagram giving explanations or commentary.

Aptitude: Defined as "capacity for learning," this is the attribute the SAT was created to measure. While it is no longer called the Scholastic Aptitude Test, the SAT is still meant to predict how well students are likely to perform in college. (It is now just the SAT Reasoning Test; the letters do not stand for anything.)

Auditory learner: Someone who learns best by hearing.

Chicago Manual of Style: An American English style guide published in 1906 by the University of Chicago Press. Its writing and citation styles are commonly used in publishing. Also known as Turabian style.

Chunking: A Reading Section test-taking strategy where a student reads a passage in chunks, moving from the passage to the answer options and back to the passage again. This process is repeated until all questions are answered.

College Board: The nonprofit organization that administers the SAT and other tests such as Advanced Placement tests. Its membership includes colleges, universities, and other educational organizations.

Diagnostic test: A full-length practice test taken in advance of the real test in order to determine what your score might be when you take the SAT.

Distractors: The industry term for incorrect answer choices. These exist to try to distract or fool the test-taker into picking them.

Documented learnings: A written list of things that you will do differently in the future based on mistakes you've made while studying for the exam.

Educated guessing: Narrowing down the provided options as much as you can before making a guess.

Free-response questions: These are the questions in the math section in which you fill in your own answer instead of choosing from a list of possible answers. These are the only questions on the test — other than the essay — that are not multiple choice.

Khan Academy: A free online resource (and partner of The College Board) that offers official, full-length practice SAT tests and study materials.

Kinesthetic learner: Someone who learns best by doing.

Lexicon: A person's vocabulary or branch of knowledge.

Mental math: Doing math in your head instead of on paper.

Morphology: The study of the form, structure, and history of words.

Percentile ranking: The number given on SAT score reports that shows the percentage of students whose score your own score exceeds on a particular section.

Process of elimination: A method used to exclude all incorrect choices in order to identify the correct one.

Quizlet: A learning website and app that can help students memorize the formulas necessary for the test.

Raw score: The actual number of questions you got right.

Scaled score: Your score after applying the scaling formula used by SAT graders.

Score Choice: A College Board program that allows test-takers to send official score reports to participating schools only from the test dates they choose. Schools that do not participate in Score Choice will see your scores from every test date when you send them official scores.

Super-score: A total SAT score built out of your best-ever scores for each section.

Test Day Kit: Should include your admit ticket, ID, snack, drink, calculator, at least five #2 pencils (sharpened) and two that are really dull, watch or timer (which must not beep or make any noise), some light reading, your keys, and your wallet.

30-second rule: If you get 30 seconds into a problem and have no idea what you are doing, cut bait and move on.

Visual learner: Someone who learns best by seeing.

Bibliography

"Application Process." *Harvard College.* The President and Fellows of Harvard College, 2016. Web. 08 Oct. 2016.

"Harvard SAT Scores and GPA." *What You Need For Harvard: SAT Scores and GPA.* PrepScholar, 2016. Web. 08 Oct. 2016.

"How Technology Impacts Sleep Quality." *Sleep. Org.* National Sleep Foundation, n.d. Web. 05 Jan. 2017.

Barron's Educational Series, Inc. *Barron's Test Prep.* **www.barronstestprep.com**.

Berkman, Justin. "How Often Is "No Error" Correct on SAT Writing?" *How Often Is "No Error" Correct on SAT Writing?* PrepScholar, 1 July 2015. Web. 10 Jan. 2017.

Browsh, Alexis. "SAT Prep Advice." E-mail interview. 9 Oct. 2016.

Chemical Heritage Foundation. "Joseph Priestley." *Chemical Achievers.* **www.chemheritage.org.**

Cheng, Allen. "How to Get 800 on SAT Reading: 11 Strategies by a Perfect Scorer." *How to Get 800 on SAT Reading: 11 Strategies by a Perfect Scorer.* PrepScholar, 28 Feb. 2015. Web. 10 Jan. 2017.

CollegeBoard. "SAT Fee Waivers." *SAT Suite of Assessments.* CollegeBoard, 12 Sept. 2016. Web. 22 Oct. 2016

CollegeBoard. "SAT." *Suite of Assessments.* CollegeBoard, 11 Oct. 2016. Web. 22 Oct. 2016.

CollegeBoard. "Scoring Your SAT® Practice Test #1." *Scoring Your SAT® Practice Test #1.* CollegeBoard, 4 Aug. 2015. Web. 16 Oct. 2016.

Flannigan, Kevin. "Building a Better Vocabulary." *Audible.com.* The Great Courses, 2015. Web. 20 Jan. 2017.

Green, Sharon Weiner and Ira Wolf. (2006). *Barron's How to Prepare for the SAT 2007.* New York: Barron's Educational Series, Inc.

Kahn Academy. "Planning Your SAT Practice." *Khan Academy.* Khan Academy, 2016. Web. 22 Oct. 2016.

Kornblum, Janet and Greg Toppo. (2008, April 25). "Studies: SAT writing portion good predictor of grades." *USA Today.*

Kukuxumusu S.L. "The Running of the Bulls." **www.sanfermin.com.**

Lemann, Nicholas. (1999). *The Big Test: The Secret History of the American Meritocracy.* New York: Farrar Straus and Giroux.

Lindsay, Samantha. "How Long Should I Study for the SAT? 6 Step Guide." *PrepScholar.* PrepScholar, 14 May 2015. Web. 28 Sept. 2016.

McIlvaine, Alexandra. "SAT Prep Advice." E-mail interview. 29 Sept. 2016.

Rose, Tom. "SAT Prep Advice." E-mail interview. 29 Sept. 2016.

Schaeffer, Bob. "Flaws in the New SAT." *The New York Times.* The New York Times, 15 Feb. 2016. Web. 22 Oct. 2016.

Steen, Clark. "SAT Prep Advice." E-mail interview. 28 Sept. 2016.

The College Board. "SAT Preparation Center." **www.collegeboard. com**.

The College Board. (2005). *The Official SAT Study Guide.* New York: College Board SAT.

Winerip, Michael. (2005, May 4). "SAT Essay Test Rewards Length and Ignores Errors." *The New York Times.*

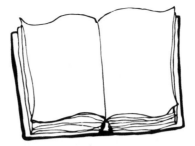

Index